FUTURE
PAST

A NOVEL

**ADAPTED FROM THE GRAPHIC NOVEL
BY CHRIS CLAREMONT AND JOHN BYRNE**

MARVEL

X-MEN: DAYS OF FUTURE PAST

A NOVEL OF THE MARVEL UNIVERSE

ALEX IRVINE

X-MEN: DAYS OF FUTURE PAST PROSE NOVEL MASS MARKET PAPERBACK. Published by MARVEL WORLDWIDE, INC., a subsidiary of MARVEL ENTERTAINMENT, LLC. OFFICE OF PUBLICATION: 135 West 50th Street, New York, NY 10020. Copyright © 2016 MARVEL

ISBN# 978-0-7851-8976-3

Printed in the U.S.A.

ALAN FINE, President, Marvel Entertainment; DAN BUCKLEY, President, TV, Publishing & Brand Management; JOE QUESADA, Chief Creative Officer; TOM BREVOORT, SVP of Publishing; DAVID BOGART, SVP of Business Affairs & Operations, Publishing & Partnership; C.B. CEBULSKI, VP of Brand Management & Development, Asia; DAVID GABRIEL, SVP of Sales & Marketing, Publishing; JEFF YOUNGQUIST, VP of Production & Special Projects; DAN CARR, Executive Director of Publishing Technology; ALEX MORALES, Director of Publishing Operations; SUSAN CRESPI, Production Manager; STAN LEE, Chairman Emeritus. For information regarding advertising in Marvel Comics or on Marvel.com, please contact Vit DeBellis, Integrated Sales Manager, at vdebellis@marvel.com. For Marvel subscription inquiries, please call 888-511-5480. **Manufactured between 3/4/2016 and 4/11/2016 by SHERIDAN, CHELSEA, MI, USA.**

First printing 2016
10 9 8 7 6 5 4 3 2 1

INTERIOR AND COVER ART BY JOHN BYRNE AND TERRY AUSTIN

Stuart Moore, Editor
Design by Nelson Ribeiro
Production by Joe Frontirre

VP, Production & Special Projects: Jeff Youngquist
Associate Editor: Sarah Brunstad
SVP Print, Sales & Marketing: David Gabriel
Editor In Chief: Axel Alonso
Chief Creative Officer: Joe Quesada
Publisher: Dan Buckley
Executive Producer: Alan Fine

Acknowledgments

Thanks first to Chris Claremont and John Byrne for the original story that gave me so much to work with in this adaptation. Also thanks to Stuart Moore, Jeff Youngquist, and Sarah Brunstad for clear-eyed reading and editing. They made the book better. A conversation with Daniel Ketchum on a completely unrelated topic sparked some interesting ideas about Magneto that I tried to put to good use. And of course, as always, thanks to Lindsay for being there and being swell.

X-MEN:
DAYS OF FUTURE PAST

A NOVEL OF THE MARVEL UNIVERSE

CHAPTER 1

COLD wind blew from the north down the deserted stretch of Park Avenue, somewhere in the East Seventies. Kate Pryde remembered walking these streets with the X-Men as a girl—she'd been, what, thirteen when she first joined up?

A lot had changed in the last twenty years. Everything had started to fall apart so fast after she joined the X-Men. The Brotherhood had assassinated Senator Kelly, Charles Xavier and Moira MacTaggert had died not long after, and Project Wideawake had quickly set off the long tragic slide to the present.

The past was past. There was no changing it. She—like every other mutant still living under Sentinel rule—couldn't afford to look back or look forward. All they could do was try to survive every day.

But maybe, just maybe, they were about to change that. She and Ororo and Peter, Franklin and Rachel and Magneto.

And Logan. It all depended on Logan.

Kate picked up her pace. She'd hurried through her delivery, trying to get ahead of schedule so the Sentinels wouldn't be suspicious of her. They could track the location of her inhibitor collar, so she didn't dare take the shortest route between Hunter College and the bus stop at Fifth and 79th, where she could board and ride back to the South Bronx. The buses didn't stop on every block like they used to, and most of the subways weren't running at all. It was a death sentence for mutants to travel alone through the disused tunnels—or most other places in the city. They were safer in the camp.

This particular neighborhood was hardcore Rogue territory. The Rogues were a criminal Mafia now, more or less, but they had their beginnings in the organized anti-mutant militias of the 2020s. Of all the places in the city for

Logan to want to meet, he had to pick Rogue territory. It made a kind of sense, since the Sentinels didn't even bother monitoring this part of the city. The Rogues did their work for them here. New York was honeycombed with underground warrens and tunnel complexes—it always had been. And now, with the Sentinels patrolling the surface, underground pathways were even more important. The Rogues controlled many of the subterranean crossroads in this part of Manhattan. They didn't like the Sentinels, but they liked mutants even less.

Kate was breathing hard, having run for the past half-mile or more to get ahead of schedule so her planned stop wouldn't make her late. This part of Park Avenue had been the scene of a number of guerrilla battles, back when people were still resisting the Sentinels. Now it was strewn with wreckage and rubble. Parts of the sidewalk were gone—the gaps overlaid with sheets of plywood, corrugated roofing, anything people could find. Kate crept along the edge of one of those sheets, testing each step as she went. New York City, once one of human-kind's great achievements, was now an endless series of lethal booby traps—especially for a mutant alone.

That was what Sentinel rule had done. Ruth-lessly adhering to their mutant-control directive, they had crushed any and all resistance, destroy-ing large swathes of cities to root out their en-emies and leaving the rest lawless ruins. The majority of mutants were dead, and most of the rest had been relegated to the South Bronx in-ternment camp Kate was returning to now. Only one, as far as she knew, was still at large, but how long would it be until the Sentinels rounded up Logan, too? There weren't enough mutants left to make a difference to their own fate. At least that was how it seemed most of the time.

But maybe they were about to do something about that. She didn't dare hope, exactly, but for the first time in years Kate Pryde could under-stand not being hopeless. Not everyone hated mutants. Not everyone believed in the Sentinels' plan. Not everyone—

Kate's foot caught on a broken board, and she stumbled. The plywood sheet under her foot gave and tilted spilling her not into a hole, but down a steep ramp into darkness. She tumbled and landed hard, realizing that she'd walked into a trap. And in Rogue territory, that could mean only one thing:

The three men looking at her from the other side of the room were Rogues, and she was in a lot of trouble.

She was in some kind of living space, with filthy mattresses along the walls. The three men stood, looking at her with malevolent glee, around a tabletop covered with the remains of a thousand melted candles. The walls were lined with rusted and bent metal shelving units, some of which still had ancient canned goods on them. The toxins in those cans had probably mutated to the point where they could have joined the X-Men—had there still been X-Men to join.

"Hey, look what we got here," one of the men said. The Rogues were known to costume themselves in outrageous ways; this one wore a Mohawk, feathers in his hair, and face paint. He was flanked by a Mad Hatter and a bedraggled-looking frontier type, both with clubs. "Little mutie tripped and fell. What are you doing out of the camp, little mutie?"

"Sentinel business," she said, not that it would do any good.

It was true. She was returning from a delivery. She had permission from the Sentinels.

What she had delivered were samples of mutant tissue. Where she had delivered them to was an experimental facility built into what had once been a science lab at Hunter College. It was still a science lab, but the people working there now weren't professors. They were handpicked by the Sentinels for two qualities: scientific expertise and implacable hostility toward mutants.

The latter was a quality the Rogues shared. All three of them were looking at the inhibitor collar exposed when her coat had come open during her tumble down the ramp.

"Inhibitor collar says you're fair game, little mutie," the Mad Hatter said. All three men stepped closer, closing the ring around Kate. "And even if you are on Sentinel business, we hate them almost as much as we hate you."

Mohawk took a step in front of the other two, leering at her. "Beg all you want, sweetheart. Scream all you want. Even if people hear, no one's coming to help you." He took another step. "You're gonna be a long time dyin', mutie."

Maybe so, Kate thought. But I'm not just going to let it happen.

Expecting her to be cowed, Mohawk came a little too close. Kate—her long-ago Danger Room training still deep in her muscle memory—snapped a straight kick right up into his gut, aiming for the bundle of nerves at the solar plexus. She made solid contact; Mohawk whoofed out air and doubled over, dropping to his knees. A crash sounded from behind him, somewhere in the darkness beyond the reach of the candles on the table. Then a second sound, a meaty crunch she recognized all too well from the violence she'd witnessed in recent years. Were the other two fighting over something? Over *her*?

Kate scrambled backward away from Mohawk. On his hands and knees, he growled, "Robbo, George—get her. Hold her. I'm gonna flay this mutie alive, and then the fun's gonna start."

"No you're not, bub," came a new voice in the room, and from the darkness stepped Logan. He kicked aside the unconscious Mad Hatter's top hat; it rolled around in a curve to bump up against the equally unconscious prospector. "You're gonna step back from the lady or join your two pals here in the land of traumatic brain injuries."

Relief crashed over Kate when she saw Logan. He'd tracked her—he must have. But had the Sentinels tracked *him*? If he hadn't used his claws, they wouldn't have noticed any mutant activi—unless they'd developed some new surveillance tech. She didn't know. They were always creating new ways to find and kill mutants…and mutant sympathizers, or anyone else they thought might oppose their plans.

"You giving Big Alex orders? On his own turf? Is that what you're doing, short stuff?" Mohawk drew a knife. "Cool. I like to earn my fun. You want the little mutie, old man, you come get her."

"If you say so," Logan said. "But don't say I didn't warn you." He stepped forward to meet Big Alex.

Kate's heart jumped into her throat when she saw his hands drop to waist level and his fists turn over, just as he always had right before unsheathing his claws. No, Logan, she thought. Don't do it. You'll bring the Sentinels! But there was no *snikt*, and no claws. Old habits—in Logan's case, nearly two hundred years old—were hard, but not impossible, to break.

Big Alex took a swipe with his knife, all ferocity and no skill. Logan angled his body just enough for the blade's edge to pass an inch from his chin. His weight shifted to one leg and the other came up in a sweeping kick that knocked the knife from Big Alex's hand. The Rogue's momentum was still carrying him forward, and Logan treated him to an elbow on his way by. The impact on the back of Big Alex's head made Kate a little sick to her stomach. As Big Alex went down, Logan turned, dropped to drive a knee into the small of his back, and delivered two more punches whose impact Kate couldn't see but could hear all too clearly.

Then he stood up, rolled his shoulders to loosen them up, and turned around. "You okay, Kate?"

She stood. "I'm fine. But calls this close, I can live without."

"I know what you mean." He looked up the ramp and listened for a moment. "Come on. Let's roll."

When they were out on the street again, Kate started to relax—at least as much as a mutant in New York, under Sentinel control, could ever relax. "So tell me, Colonel Logan. How's life in the Canadian Resistance Army?"

"Thrill a minute, darlin'," Logan said. "The word from London is that everything's on automatic. The minute the Sentinels start to move out of North America, every nuclear power is going to launch a full-scale strike."

"Then it's up to the X-Men," Kate said. It felt good to say it, as if the words could give the X-Men the power they'd once had.

"As always, right?" Logan held out his hand, palm up, displaying a small machined piece of metal. It was a short tube with a set of coils around its middle and a disc attached to one side of the coils. "Here you go. Last bit of the Jammer. The FCA eggheads made it out of an alloy that shouldn't show up on Sentinel scanners. You oughta be able to walk right into the camp with it."

"Easy for you to say."

"Sure is," Logan agreed. "Phase Two begins at midnight sharp. You'll see the sign I left. Be ready."

"We will." She paused, not quite ready to leave him yet. Seeing a free mutant was wonderful, inspiring even, but knowing she would soon be walking back through the gates of the camp made Kate want to run away. Maybe to Canada. But she couldn't leave her friends. As she had said, it was up to the X-Men.

"You think this will work?" she asked, just to keep the conversation going a little longer.

"It better," Logan said. "There're a thousand warheads pointed at us, and some itchy trigger fingers on their buttons. The second Europe thinks the Sentinels are moving out past North America, we're gonna be so much ash up in the jetstream."

Something about this image struck Kate. It reminded her of her life before the inhibitor collar, when she had been able to phase. The feeling of individual molecules passing through her body, the incredible rush of knowing you could do something that maybe only one other person in the world could do.

A lot had changed.

Maybe they could change it back.

"Get on home, little Kit," Logan said. "You don't want the Sentinels looking at you too close."

Kate zipped up her camp jumpsuit over the Jammer component, tucked into a tear in the inside lining. "We won't get another chance, will we?"

"Nope. If this doesn't work, we're all gonna die, kid. Simple as that."

She nodded.

"That's why it has to work." Logan climbed up onto the street and reached down to give Kate a hand up. "Catch you later," he said. "You know when and where."

Again she nodded. She was dying to talk about it, but they'd already said more than was prudent, given the possibility of Sentinel surveillance.

Kate felt Logan's eyes on her as she walked the last few blocks to the bus station across Fifth Avenue from Central Park, where the 79th Street transverse road disappeared into the forest. It had been a long time, more than a decade, since New York City had last maintained the park. The buses themselves hadn't run on diesel or natural gas or electricity for about that long. Now they were pulled by teams of horses.

She boarded a bus and instinctively looked for a spot away from other passengers. She was keenly aware not just of her inhibitor collar, but also of her camp coverall which bore a large black M on the back branding her as a mutant. The Sentinels and their human abettors had issued classifications as part of the Mutant Control Act of 2019. "H" meant regular "Human," free of active mutations or genetic predisposition to them. This group didn't have to dress or conduct themselves in any particular way, but many of them wore a block H on their clothing as a mark of pride and genetic purity. "A" stood for "Anomalous," a category of people whose genomes contained the potential for active mutations. As could not breed and were required to display their letter.

And then there was "M." The only time an M was seen in the general populace was when the Sentinels sent one on a specific errand, as they had Kate. She heard the remarks as she boarded; she found no seat because everyone on the bus, H and A alike, spread out to prevent her from sitting nearby. This was partly human cruelty, but it was also a protective act. The Sentinels monitored interactions between mutants and other people, and Sentinel suspicion was something to be avoided at all costs.

So Kate stood watching the city go by at a horse's walking pace, taking care to avoid eye contact with her fellow passengers. Attacks on mutants outside the camp were rare, but only because it was highly unusual for a mutant to be granted the privilege of exiting the base. Kate held that privilege dear, both because it was necessary to the plan and because it gave her a chance to see what was becoming of the United States of America. On the other hand, if that plan worked, she would never have need of her exit privileges again.

She looked up at the sky, dreary and spitting

rain, and imagined what it might look like when the warheads began to fall.

In Canada, according to Logan, things were a little better—but only because Canadian mutants had seen what was coming, soon after Project Wideawake went active. They'd had time to plan, to get out of the cities and make themselves as hard to find as possible. Logan didn't share much with Kate because neither of them knew when the Sentinels might interrogate her, but she had gathered from passing references that the Canadian super-team Alpha Flight might still be alive and active, somewhere northwest of the Great Lakes.

Not that Alpha Flight could do her any good from that far away. If the fragmentary remains of the once-proud X-Men were going to stave off a nuclear devastation of North America, they would have to do it from the South Bronx.

CHAPTER 2

KATE got off the bus near Yankee Stadium and crossed the parking lots to the camp gates, where two Sentinels stood guard. The first spoke as she approached. "Mutant 187, you are behind schedule. Explain."

"I was attacked by Rogues on Park Avenue," she said, choosing her words carefully to keep the Sentinels' sensors from detecting hesitation or omission. She'd rehearsed possible responses for days, anticipating this scenario. "I escaped. That caused the delay."

"Encephalo-scan indicates truthful response. Proceed." Luckily for Kate, the Sentinel did not interrogate her further. It would have been very easy to get caught in a lie, which would likely mean execution on the spot. If the Sentinel were even slightly uncertain, it would subject her to a process of exhaustive and humiliating interrogations that might uncover the Jammer component. That would end the plan before it ever had a chance to begin.

But none of that happened. Quit with the flights of fancy, she told herself. You don't need to imagine alternative futures—you're about to live one.

At least she hoped she was. The next few hours would tell most of that story, one way or another.

Once she had passed through the security checkpoint at the gate, Kate walked along the fence line, staying away from the maze-like interior of the camp. It was dangerous in there. At the time of its construction, the camp had been organized into three sections. The first, near the front gates, consisted of a group of low buildings housing a research lab, medical facilities, and administrative offices.

Most of the original mutant inmates were now in the cemetery that occupied part of the space between the administrative complex and

the main body of the camp. Here, a long double row of barracks stood in front of crumbling
row houses. The whole capacity of the place had
never been dedicated to mutants: From the beginning, it had also housed normal-human re-
sisters and various other unfortunates deemed
undesirable by the Sentinels. Some of these
were members of anti-mutant groups whose
violent tendencies put them on the wrong side
of the Sentinels' desire for order. Theoretical-
ly, they were not supposed to come into contact
with the dwindling number of mutant inmates.
In practice, the Sentinels looked the other way.
A number of the mutants buried in the cemetery
had died at the hands of other inmates. The most
recent casualty had been Kurt Wagner, the mutant called Nightcrawler, just a year or so before.

After that incident, the Sentinels had confined the mutants to a single building in one corner of the camp, where sentries could keep a
closer eye on them. Eventually, Kate knew, the
Sentinels would achieve whatever research goal

they had set themselves, and then they would kill the remaining mutants. Until then, however, the mutants had their own housing, with its own kitchen to keep them out of the camp dining area.

The original barracks buildings had been modified over the years, their clean, regular lines transformed into a jumble of makeshift barriers, catwalks, tunnels, and covered passages that reflected the Balkanization of the camp population. The nonmutant inmates came from various gangs and groups on the outside, and they brought those affiliations in with them. The Sentinels didn't care unless violence broke out; when it did, their reprisals were swift and brutal. Several times since Kate had been brought to the camp, Sentinels had burned part of it down. Then the inmates rebuilt—further altering the original, orderly layout.

Just as no mutant would willingly go into Rogue territory on the outside, no mutant would willingly enter that warren. Kate headed for the medical facility, sticking to the open spaces within sight of the Sentinel guards posted along the fence. She walked by Kurt's grave, and tried not to look at all the others. The past was past. She had to stay focused on the future—on making sure they would *have* one.

She returned the medical case to the camp infirmary, where the doctors dismissed her without looking her in the eye. To them, she was subhuman, an aberrant strain, a genetic dead end soon to be eliminated from the species. Maybe some of them didn't believe that, but in the camp it didn't matter what you believed. What mattered were your actions, and the H-class humans who worked for the Sentinels were utterly complicit in the ongoing mutant genocide in North America. Thinking of it made Kate wonder whether maybe Magneto hadn't been right all along.

On the other hand, Magneto himself had traded in his former militancy for a weary, plodding cynicism. Mutants were too few and too far gone, perhaps, to believe that militant action would do any good.

Unless the Jammer worked. It was their last chance.

The rest of the X-Men…Kate caught herself. It was easy to think of them still as the X-Men. But wasn't that a dead appellation for a dead group, from a dead history? The X-Men had died when Charles Xavier died, really. Now they were just the rest of the surviving mutants, the last great hope of mutantkind in North America and maybe the world. And they were waiting for her in their small prefabricated sheet-metal barracks.

She stepped inside and immediately felt safer among her friends.

First to meet her inside the door was Ororo Munroe, Kate's guiding light when she'd first come to the X-Men all those years ago. The intervening years showed in a slight rounding of Ororo's features and figure—but she was still strong and graceful, with an air of calm command that belied her X-Men name: Storm. Just behind her came Franklin Richards who, having reached middle age, had the same pattern of gray at his temples as his late father, Reed Richards of the Fantastic Four.

Rachel Summers looked up from a table in the common space just inside the front doorway. Her red hair had been chopped raggedly short by her own hand; her face was perpetually drawn and pale, as if she hadn't had a good night's sleep in decades. Rachel was a mystery to the rest of them—even Franklin, whom Rachel had married soon after being imprisoned. Kate knew nothing about Rachel's past, which seemed to be a forbidden topic of discussion. This had always struck her as unfair: Rachel was a telepath and therefore had probably learned everything there was to know about the rest of them before the Sentinels had forced an inhibitor collar on her.

Hanging back from the group was Magneto in his wheelchair. He'd been crippled by a Sentinel raid on his secret base in the Caribbean, during which all of his closest Brotherhood lieutenants had been killed. He looked much the same as he always had, Kate thought—his face lined, and his unruly shock of gray hair never changing. It was odd to see, in light of how the others had aged.

And next to Magneto stood Kate's own husband, Peter Alexandreivich Rasputin. It had been a long time since anyone called him Colossus. Kate went to Peter and leaned into him, taking comfort as she always did from his size and his calm demeanor. Even when he wasn't transformed into shining organic steel—as he had not done for many years—he was still a mountainous presence.

"Sorry I'm late," she said. "I ran into a Rogue pack. They ran into Wolverine." Concern passed across Peter's face at the mention of Rogues, but disappeared at the mention of Wolverine.

"He didn't do anything…?" Ororo let the question hang.

"No, nothing that would draw the Sentinels' attention," Kate said. "Logan's smarter than that."

"It's not his intelligence I question, Kate," Ororo said. "I question his temper."

"Well, I have the final module," Kate said. "Logan's going to do his part at midnight, like we talked about. Phase One has to be complete by then."

"Phase One," Peter said. "How normal we make it sound, yet what we contemplate is so fantastic. I still cannot believe it is possible."

"Strange words, Piotr Alexandreivich, coming from one who's seen and done the things you have." Magneto moved his wheelchair slowly across the broken asphalt. He was no longer an enemy—there were too few mutants left to permit differences among them—but he still stayed apart from the other five. Old separations, old enmities, took even longer than twenty years to fully die out.

Peter chuckled. "I have ever been a simple man, old friend. More farmer in my soul than super hero."

"That may be what we need: a little touch of the New Soviet Man," Magneto said. "Optimism. The will to move forward no matter what the cost. If there were any alternative, we would take it. But if we do nothing, the world will be at war by tomorrow. By the day after…North America will be craters and ashes. Our actions may not make things better, either for us or for humanity as a whole, but we certainly cannot make them worse."

How easily he slipped into the role of leader, Kate noted. He spoke for them all, incorporated their concerns and fears, turned them into strength. No wonder he had been such a dangerous enemy.

"Rachel," he was saying, wheeling himself closer to her and Franklin. "So much depends on you tonight."

"I won't fail, Magneto," she said. "I've been meditating all day. Once the Jammer's operational, we can start anytime."

"Then what are we waiting for?" Kate blurted out. She immediately regretted her tone—she hadn't meant to snap at anyone, but her nerves were getting the better of her, especially after her encounter with the Rogues. The plan depended on her as much as it did on Rachel, and the waiting—the endless preparation and speculation, the *talking*—it was killing her.

"A moment, my wife," Peter said. She stopped and turned to him. The other four moved a respectful distance away. "I have doubts. Can this work? And even if it can, should it? We are proposing to toy with the basic fabric of reality. What happens if we succeed? What might we unmake?" He took her hands, an oddly courtly gesture against the backdrop of the camp. "We ourselves—this love of ours that has survived so much—it might cease to exist along with the Sentinels."

"That's a risk we have to take, Peter," she said. "What does the love of two people matter against the lives of billions? I don't even know what will happen to the younger me. I might unmake myself. But if our love was meant to be, it will be. We must believe that. Only this time, it will be in a world where our children can grow up free and unafraid. The Sentinels killed that, along with our...our children. If changing the past holds out even the slightest hope of undoing that, I'll do it. No matter what else the cost."

His head bowed, Peter listened to her. When she was done talking, he said simply, "I love you, Kate."

"And I you, Peter...from the moment we first met."

Now he smiled. "A lovely thing to say, but you were only thirteen. Just a girl. Love—true love—comes later."

"And it will be there for us later, after I do this," Kate said. "I need you to believe that. If you don't believe it, how can I?"

"Then I will," Peter said.

An hour later, the Jammer was assembled, and they had cleared out the small room. All of them gathered briefly for a last consultation.

"We do not know—and cannot know—exactly what will happen when this projection takes place," Magneto said. "But you may be certain that the X-Men of twenty-two years ago will be highly skeptical. If I am remembering correctly, you will appear in the immediate aftermath of Jean Grey's death. The team will be grappling with that and with Scott Summers' decision to leave the X-Men for a time. Ororo, does that match your recollection?"

"Exactly," Storm said.

"Are we sure this is the best way?" Franklin asked. "Seems to me we're risking everything on a plan that—as powerful as we all know Rachel to be—really isn't likely to work."

"If you have a better idea, Franklin, we're all listening," Rachel said. He looked at her much as Peter was looking at Kate: a man uncomfortable in the knowledge that he was going to be a bystander while his wife took the lead—but also a man plainly worried for her, because none of them knew what was going to happen in the next hour. Perhaps the last hour of their lives.

"None of us has a better idea," Ororo said. "We have talked this to death. It is time to act. If we are to die, let it not be passively."

Magneto nodded. "I spent much of my child-hood in a place like this," he said. "I will not end my days in one."

Franklin held his wife's gaze a moment lon-ger. Then he held up his hands. "All right. Let's do it, then."

Magneto turned back to Rachel. "How much time do you think you need to prepare?"

"I don't know. I've never done anything like this before. A few minutes of quiet to gather my-self, then…" She took a deep breath and exhaled slowly. "Then let's try it."

"There's not going to be any trying it," Franklin said. "Either we do it or we're all dead."

"That's really helping me focus, Franklin." Rachel closed her eyes and sat still. Franklin started to say something, but Magneto held up a hand. Franklin cast a worried look back at Ra-chel, then led the others out of the room.

"Take time, Rachel," Magneto said. "But not too much. Midnight is coming, and we will only have one chance." Then he, too, was gone.

At last Rachel had a few minutes alone. She could prepare, could gather herself for a feat that even she did not know whether she could accomplish. She could ensure that Kate's persona survived the wrenching transition from this future to her teenage self, anchored twenty-two years in the past.

She could also stew over past misdeeds and perform the fruitless calculus of transgression and atonement. How many good deeds, how many lives saved, could balance the years she had spent as Ahab's hound, hunting down fugitive mutants in the early years of the Sentinel takeover?

None of the X-Men knew about her history, and Rachel wanted to keep it that way. Her sins were private. They knew her last name because the human staff of the camp used it, and Rachel had touched their minds enough to know they had drawn their own conclusions. But with so few mutants remaining, all of them knew better than to ask too many questions when the answers might create resentment and division. Sometimes she thought of telling them. It would be cathartic to unburden herself, but that benefit had to be balanced against their possible reaction upon learning she was responsible for so many of their friends' deaths.

On the other hand, she had done what she had done to survive. That was the simple truth. If it did not give her peace, at least it allowed her to live with herself.

Guilty self-examination did not do much for her concentration. Rachel sat down and focused her thoughts. She slipped into the nourishing cadence of meditative breathing and stayed there, letting only the present matter.

She had survived the massacre at Xavier's school. She had survived the purges and anti-mutant lynchings after that. She had done what she had to do to survive. And when she looked back at all those years, she could not believe that any path to redemption still lay open to her. Franklin believed in her—but perversely, that sharpened her own self-loathing. She did not deserve him. She would, she feared, fail his trust, as she had betrayed the trust of so many others before him.

Then Kate Pryde was walking back into the room, and Rachel no longer had the luxury of self-doubt.

"Are we ready?" Magneto asked, wheeling in behind Kate. Ororo, Peter, and Franklin followed behind him.

Franklin was the only one who approached Rachel. He took up a protective position behind her, hands resting on her shoulders—but she stiffened and said quietly, "I need a little space, Franklin."

He stepped back. She didn't look at him. If he was hurt, there was nothing she could do about that; knowing it would distract her.

Kitty leaned in close to Peter, who bent and kissed her once on top of her head and a second time on the lips. "Go, Kate," he said. "We will do our part. Then return to us, my love."

She nodded and walked over to the thin mattress. Here she would lie while her personality, her essence, was extracted and transmitted more than twenty years into the past.

Or she would be driven insane. Or she would die. Or her mind would arrive in a stranger's body—the possibilities for mistakes were endless.

"We've assembled the Jammer," Magneto said. "It won't work for long. Our timing must be perfect, and we're also going to need a bit of luck."

"A bit," Franklin repeated.

The Jammer sat on the floor next to the mat, at Rachel's left side; it looked a bit like a teapot on three short legs. Its case contained a small battery, a cluster of antennae, and a multi-spectrum wave interruptor. Just about any mutant power had an effect on some part of the electromagnetic spectrum, and the Sentinels were equipped with detectors keyed to the known patterns of surviving mutants. That was where the Jammer came in. It would mask the use of their abilities, permitting Rachel to perform the psychic projection. It would also let the six of them take their inhibitor collars off. Then, at least, they could put up a fight.

Kate corrected herself twice. First, only five of them would be taking off their inhibitor collars. She would be lying on the table. They'd rehearsed it, and they couldn't risk the time they'd lose getting her collar off before Rachel attempted the telepathic projection. Second, they weren't planning on putting up a fight right away. Their aim was first to escape.

Then the fight would take care of itself.

"Kate," Rachel said. "I don't have to be a telepath to know that your mind is going in every direction at once. You need to be calm and focused if this is going to work."

"Easy for you to say," Kate said. But she lay back on the table and closed her eyes, slowing her breathing and letting the chaotic swirl of her thoughts drain away until only one remained. She remembered being thirteen, the newest member of the X-Men. They had called her Sprite back then, and she hadn't had the confidence to tell Storm and the rest that she didn't like that code name very much. But she couldn't remember when she had changed it.

"Time to do this, if we're going to do it," Franklin said. He stood with one hand hovering over the Jammer's switch. "Rachel, are you ready?"

"I'm ready," she said. "But don't freak out if it doesn't happen right away. It'll probably take me a few minutes to gather Kate's consciousness and make sure I'm keeping it intact for the projection."

"We'll stay out of your way," Ororo said.

"Silence would be good," Rachel said. "Franklin, turn it on."

There was a sharp click as Franklin activated the Jammer. None of them spoke after that.

CHAPTER 3

WOLVERINE banked the Blackbird around and dropped the plane into a steep approach to the landing strip at the perimeter of the federal Max-X penitentiary, a holding facility designed for super-humans who couldn't be kept in normal prisons. The X-Men had caught an alert ninety minutes ago that some kind of explosion or possible seismic event had collapsed part of the facility. Among several possible escapees was Fred J. Dukes—better known as the Blob, one of the original members of the Brotherhood of Evil Mutants.

With the so-called "mutant hearings" on tap in the Senate the next day, Storm had immediately decided that the X-Men needed to have a strong and visible presence at the site. She, Wolverine, Nightcrawler, Colossus, and Kitty Pryde were the response team.

From the air, the prison looked at first as though a sizable bomb had destroyed one entire wing. But on closer inspection, it appeared quite different. There was no debris field scattered outward from the center of the collapse.

"Blob," Peter said. "He has grown more powerful."

Blob could increase his mass and density to the point where it was impossible to move him. He was also practically impossible to harm physically. Now it seemed he had amplified his powers, becoming dense enough that his mass could bring down any structure designed to contain him.

"He imploded the whole building?" Kurt Wagner—Nightcrawler—wondered. "*Ich staune.* Where has he gone, then?"

"Better put him underground next time," Wolverine said.

"You are a little too eager to kill, Wolverine," Peter said.

Wolverine chuckled, the sound more like a

growl than a laugh. "All I meant was if he was underground, he could drop a building on his own head and not be able to walk out. You gotta stop taking everything so seriously, Petey."

"And you should perhaps consider how your past actions make my response understandable…Logan."

Wolverine shrugged. "Fair enough. You do things your way, I do 'em mine."

"Where are all the guards?" Nightcrawler asked. Max-X was supposed to be under the control of the best soldiers a joint Special Forces-S.H.I.E.L.D. training program could produce—but the prison grounds were empty and the front gate was open. The Blackbird's radio emitted only static, even on the dedicated Max-X frequency. Something was jamming it.

The Blackbird braked to a halt on the parking lot outside the prison fence. Peter opened the fuselage door and led the way down the ramp that extended automatically below it. Storm and Nightcrawler followed, and Kitty was about to go with them when Logan cut in front of her.

"Stay on the plane, Kitten," Wolverine said. "We haven't taken the training wheels off you just yet."

"That's not fair," she protested. "I'm an X-Man. You even gave me a nickname."

"Yup, we did. So I guess I'll use it. Stay on the plane, Sprite. I'd never hear the end of it from Chuckie X if I let you out into a gunfight and something happened. Watch and learn." Wolverine held her gaze. "Got me?"

"Fine," she said, and spun away from him to go sulk in the copilot's chair.

The four X-Men crossed the parking lot, seeing right away that more was wrong than just a collapsed wing of the prison complex. Bullet holes pockmarked some of the buildings nearest the gate, which wasn't just open. It had been blown off its hinges.

"I smell blood," Logan said, just as the ambush was sprung.

The exterior doors of the prison complex

burst open. Heavily armed mercenaries bearing the blank-faced masks of the Hellfire Club poured out, guns blazing. More mercenaries appeared in the prison's sentry towers with heavier single-fire sniper rifles.

One of their shots punched through Peter's shoulder, spinning him around. He transformed into his organic-steel form, and two more bullets ricocheted off him. Nightcrawler disappeared in a puff of smoke and reappeared, saber gleaming, in the midst of one of the enemy fire teams. He took three of them down and bamfed away again before they could react.

Wolverine's approach was more straightforward: He lowered his head and charged into the midst of the closest group, claws out and slashing. Storm raised her arms and drew a fog into existence, obscuring herself as clouds appeared and darkened the sky. Rain began to fall, and a rumble of thunder echoed across the high plain.

Inside the Blackbird, Kitty Pryde watched the battle in a state of pure anguish. She *had* to do something. The X-Men had welcomed her, saved her life—and now, when they were facing overwhelming odds, she was not out there to help. She couldn't stand it. She was ready to fight. She knew it.

There were Hellfire Club mercenaries everywhere, outnumbering the X-Men by at least ten to one. But the prison guards, previously overwhelmed by the Hellfire assault, seemed emboldened by the X-Men's arrival. Gunfire sounded from within the buildings as they fought their way out and rallied to defensive positions at the edges of the prison grounds.

Colossus's organic-steel body glinted in the sunlight, sparking with the impact of dozens of bullets. They staggered him, but could not hurt him. He lowered a shoulder and barreled into the wall under one of the sentry towers, toppling it into the guardhouse close to the gate.

"Fastball Special, Petey!" Wolverine yelled, sprinting across the prison courtyard. Colossus braced his feet and caught Wolverine in mid-leap, hurling him up to somersault into the sentry tower on the other side of the gate. The Hellfire sniper got off one last shot before Wolverine struck him fists first, smashing him to the floor. A concentrated volley of machine-gun fire tore into the tower just as Logan hit the floor.

"Logan!" Kitty cried. He wasn't invincible. None of them were. She had to help. What kind of X-Man would she be if she just stood by and watched?

Kitty took a deep breath and phased, letting herself fall through the bottom of the Blackbird's fuselage and becoming solid again when her feet touched the ground. A detachment of Hellfire Club mercenaries was making a sweep around the perimeter fence, heading for the Blackbird. One of them spotted her, and she barely phased in time for their fusillade of bullets to pass through her. She resolidified and ducked behind the Blackbird's landing gear, so terrified that she couldn't even cry out. Some kind of energy blast hit the landing gear and knocked her spinning, but she kept to her feet and ran away from the Hellfire mercenaries into the pouring rain, reflexively heading for the monumental form of Colossus. He would protect her, he would—

Something hit her hard between the shoulder blades and she sprawled forward, face-down. Gasping for breath, she rolled over, waiting to see blood. Instead she saw Logan. He'd leapt from the guard tower and flattened her, absorbing the brunt of the Hellfire Club's next volley himself.

A normal man would have been shredded, but Wolverine was just mad. He tore into the Hellfire mercenaries and put the six of them down before Kitty managed to get back to her feet.

Covered in blood and still snarling, he turned to her. "I told you, Kit, stay on the blasted plane. You're not ready for this yet." He was pointing at her; when he saw her staring at the blood on his claws, he drew them in. "Kit, you gotta listen—hey!"

Something else hit Kitty then, an upheaval in her mind that tore her loose from her senses and dropped her into darkness.

LOGAN saw Kitty go down. He spun around in a full circle. There were no other Hellfire mercenaries nearby. He hadn't heard a shot except those coming from inside the complex, where the S.H.I.E.L.D. guards were regaining the upper hand.

Nightcrawler bamfed into existence next to him. "*Was ist los?*"

"She just dropped," Logan said, kneeling over Kitty. She was breathing, and he couldn't see any wounds.

"I will tell Ororo," Nightcrawler said, disappearing in a puff of brimstone.

Well, damn, Logan thought. Now I'm babysitting?

Not for long, as it turned out. Logan and Colossus had already reduced the number of Hellfire Club mercenaries by more than half. Now, not ten seconds after Nightcrawler had vanished, a bolt of lightning blasted out of the sky, forking to strike the four remaining sentry towers and the perimeter fence to take out most of the Hellfire mercenaries who had the misfortune to be outside. In the ozone-smelling aftermath, the remaining mercenaries surrendered en masse.

For another few moments, gunshots sounded from inside the complex. Then the S.H.I.E.L.D. guards who had survived the initial attack emerged from their defensive position to gather the prisoners, freeing Colossus to turn his attention to Kitty and Logan.

"She's out cold, but she doesn't look hurt," Logan said. "I don't know what the hell happened."

"I will stay with her," Colossus said.

Logan took off, finishing the sweep of the Max-X grounds to see whether any of the other superhuman inmates had escaped. Along the way, he released some guards he found trapped in a partially collapsed wing of the main complex.

"You men better make sure the rest of your guests are still here," he said.

Then he hurried to catch up with Ororo and Kurt. They were out near the prison's main gate, consulting with the warden, a career S.H.I.E.L.D. officer named Yargeau with a gash splitting his crew cut and a nose clearly just broken during the fight. "Blob had his lawyer in yesterday," Yargeau was saying. "First we knew he had a lawyer—but hey, it's America. They talked for about an hour, and then she left. Nothing unusual."

"That's something unusual," Logan said, and pointed.

They all looked—and then they all froze.

The Sentinel descended, slowly and precisely, from the skies over the southern Rockies. Keeping itself oriented toward the Blackbird, it touched down on the bare ground between the runway and the collapsed portion of the Max-X complex. Then it stood watchful and still. It was one of the older models, perhaps rolled out by the Master Mold itself. Every mutant watching it got an uneasy sensation, all the way down in the base of the brain, the place where the fight-or-flight response lived. That was what Sentinels meant to them.

Logan started walking toward it. "Sentinel on the grounds. There's more goin' on here than just a jailbreak."

"Colonel?" Storm prompted. "Is there anything you want to tell me?"

"Never seen it here before," Yargeau said. "Or any Sentinel. S.H.I.E.L.D. doesn't use them. You guys know that."

"Drawn by us using our powers, no doubt," she said. "Let's see what it has to say for itself."

She called Logan back. Of all the team, he was the most likely to lose his temper.

It had been some time since the X-Men had seen an active Sentinel. As Storm rose to its eye level, the Sentinel made no move to attack. An arc of static electricity snapped between them as she hovered perhaps ten feet from it. "Sentinel. Why are you here?"

"To observe mutants."

"Plenty of us to observe," Wolverine said.

"To observe only?" Storm prompted.

"The nature of my orders is not to be disseminated to unauthorized parties," the Sentinel said.

"And who are the authorized parties?"

"The roster of authorized parties is not to be disseminated to unauthorized parties."

"We should take it out, 'Ro," Wolverine said.

"Expression of hostile intent detected," the Sentinel said. "Threat assessment under way."

"There is no threat," Storm said. "We are only here to pursue the escaped prisoner Fred Dukes."

"Observations will continue," the Sentinel said. "Detection of hostile intent mandates ongoing threat assessment until confirmation of secure environment."

Yargeau stepped forward. "Robot, I hear you talking about authorization, but I didn't authorize you being here. Nobody at S.H.I.E.L.D. did. Get off this property before we do our own threat assessment."

"Expression of hostile intent detected," the Sentinel said, this time looking down at Yargeau. "Source nonmutant. Threat dismissed."

"Is that right," Yargeau said.

Storm landed next to the S.H.I.E.L.D. officer. "Your support is noted and appreciated, Colonel

Yargeau," she said. "But let's not escalate this confrontation."

"If that's how you want to play it, Miss Munroe," Yargeau said with a last sharp gaze at the Sentinel. "But my superiors are going to hear about this. I will not have this at my facility."

Two of his subordinates approached him with preliminary damage and casualty reports. "Blob's the only escapee," one of them said. "This whole thing was targeted to him, looks like."

"Let's make sure," Yargeau said. "Count again. And the minute we get power restored, everything's on lockdown until further notice. Your lightning did a number on our electrical grid."

"Next time we'll save your wiring and let the Hellfire Club ruin the place, maybe," Wolverine said.

"Enough, Logan," Storm said. "Colonel Yargeau, I'm sure you can appreciate that this kind of battle sometimes requires the use of blunt instruments. We'll be on our way soon. Blob will not have gotten far on his own. If he is in the vicinity, we will find him; if not, we will know there was some kind of coordinated effort to extract him."

"By whom, is the question," Nightcrawler said. "Has the Brotherhood re-formed?"

"We'll know soon enough," Storm said. "Right now we've got a more pressing issue. Peter, what's Kitty's status?"

"She's starting to come around," Peter answered.

He helped Kitty to a sitting position. She opened her eyes and started to focus on her surroundings. Joy chased shock across her face as she saw the X-Men.

"Kurt! You're alive!" she cried out.

It flooded over her, everything at once. The shock of clean air and bright sun, after long years in the polluted ruins of New York. The sensory feedback of her body, thirteen years old, before the decades of fighting and deprivation that had left their traces even on her resilient mutant physiology. She felt so light, so full of energy.

Even colors seemed more vibrant, from the lustrous green of the shrubs lining the runway to the rich dark blue of Nightcrawler's skin…

In a sharp dissonant moment she remembered him dead, lying in the mud at the edge of the camp's barracks, rain falling on his face. But here he was, now, a wry puzzled smile on his face as he reacted to her words.

"So it would appear, my kitten," he replied. "Was there ever any doubt?"

She scrambled to her feet—how light she was, how nimble!—and looked around. "Where are we? This isn't New York."

"Closest town is Demming, New Mexico," Wolverine said.

"Oh, I thought—" Kate looked down at herself, confirming with her eyes what her nervous system had already told her. "I'm thirteen," she said wonderingly. "It worked!" Then she spun around to fling herself into Colossus' arms. "Peter…"

"Yes, Kitty." Peter looked uncomfortable at the intensity of her reaction.

Storm stepped closer and put a hand on Kate's shoulder. "Kitty, are you all right? Did you hit your head? Did something happen?"

Did it ever, Kate thought. It was time to get a grip on herself and get on with the mission. There was no time to waste, either here or back in her future. "You're never going to believe this," she said, reluctantly separating herself from Peter, "but I'm not Kitty. I'm Kate."

"She did hit her head. Must've," Wolverine said.

They had all warned her to keep her cool when the X-Men in the past didn't believe her, but Kate could already feel the first hints of frustration. She tried to stay focused. "No, Logan, it's…I can't believe it worked. This is going to sound crazy, but I'm not Kitty. At least I haven't gone by that name in a long time…since just a few years from now."

"We must get her to a medical facility," Peter said.

"No, Peter, I'm fine, listen. I'm…I mean,

this is my thirteen-year-old body, but I'm Kate. I'm thirty-five, and my mind has been sent back through time to warn you. There's a terrible future…" She looked again at Nightcrawler. Almost more than the proprioceptive shock of being in her adolescent body again, the sight of him was hard to wrap her head around. "Kurt, I saw you die. It was…"

Storm was looking more and more concerned. "Your first combat experience can be a shock," she said gently. "That's why we wanted you to stay on the Blackbird. We thought it best for you to just observe until you had progressed a little further in your Danger Room training."

"The Danger Room," Kate repeated. She hadn't thought of it in…well, years. "So Professor Xavier…he's still alive?"

"He's in Washington about to testify before the Senate," Storm said. "He's very much alive, yes."

"That's exactly why I'm here!" Kate said. "The Senate! The Brotherhood is going to attack the hearing and assassinate Senator Kelly—and

Professor Xavier, and Moira! When that happens, a whole new series of Sentinels are going to be unleashed, and in twenty years there won't be a dozen mutants left alive in North America."

"Paranoia worthy of Magneto," Nightcrawler commented. "Our Kitten is scared out of her mind."

"Yes, I am. And you would be too, if you'd seen what I've seen. We live in an internment camp in the Bronx. The Sentinels are almost finished with their work. You have to believe me! If we don't do something, the professor and Senator Kelly will be dead by the end of the day, and it'll be too late to change anything." She turned to Kurt, talking fast. She had to get it all out, all at once. "You mentioned Magneto. He's still alive, but crippled. He's in a wheelchair, but he helped Rachel prepare to send me back. She's the only telepath left."

"Who's Rachel?" Storm asked.

Seizing on this tiny expression of belief, Kate whirled back to Storm. "Rachel Summers.

She's Scott's, Cyclops', daughter. Where is Scott, anyway—oh. Right. I remember. Jean."

"Yeah. Jean," Wolverine said. "Cyke is taking himself a little mental-health sabbatical. We all could use one after the Dark Phoenix business but hey, someone has to mind the store. Also, you know Scotty doesn't have any kids, right?"

"Let her talk, Logan," Storm warned.

"Scott dies," Kate said. "Not right away. Later, when the Sentinels really take over."

"How 'bout the rest of us?" Wolverine asked.

"Storm and Peter are still alive. You too, Logan. You're the only one who's not in the camp. Also Magneto's there, like I said, and Franklin."

"Franklin Richards?" Storm said.

Kate nodded. Every question they asked gave her a little more hope that they were starting to believe her. "But Reed and Sue are both gone, along with Ben and Johnny. The Sentinels didn't just kill a few mutants. They decided the best way to control the mutant threat was to eliminate all opposition. There's a graveyard in the camp—I walk by it every day."

She looked around. "This feels so strange," she said. "To be only thirteen again…and to know everything that's going to happen to all of us…" Her gaze lingered on Peter for a long moment.

"What—"

But Peter never got to finish his question. Over his shoulder, Kate saw the Sentinel.

Oh no, she thought. Something went wrong. This is the wrong past. The Sentinels are already loose…

It was too much, on top of the Rogue attack and the unfamiliarity of everything around her. Seeing the Sentinel triggered an ingrained flight reflex. She screamed and turned to run, plowing straight into Logan, who caught her in a bear hug. "Whoa, Kit!" he said. But she phased right through him and ran blindly away from the Sentinel, across the cleared ground toward the brushy hills. Anywhere to escape the Sentinel.

Nightcrawler teleported into her path, and she ran into him, staggering him as he tried to hold on to her.

"*Ruh, Kätzchen,*" he said. "You're safe, you're safe—" And then she phased through him too, sinking up to her waist in the rocky ground and scrambling back to the surface. Night-crawler caught her again, and again she phased through him. Storm swooped overhead, unable to help. Kate and Kurt hopscotched across the open ground in a series of brimstone-scented collisions until she exhausted herself and collapsed, with him kneeling at her side.

"The Sentinels," she said. "They're already here. I…for a minute I thought…"

Storm landed next to them and crouched alongside Kurt. "Kitten, Kitten," she said. "You've had a shock. Try to calm yourself."

"I'm not Kitten! I'm Kate!" she cried out. "Don't tell me to be calm! You don't know what they've done!"

Logan and Peter caught up to the three of them, and stood looking down at her. She had to get herself under control. They were never going to believe her if she couldn't handle herself. "Give her a moment," Storm said.

"What do you mean about the Sentinels?" Logan asked. "It's weird that one showed up here, but that's the only one I've seen lately. They're not doing anything."

"They're not?" Kate took a deep breath. She had to not panic. She had to focus. But it wasn't easy, with the stress of her last few hours now being routed through the hormonal hair trigger of adolescence. This was part of the projection that she had considered intellectually without really being prepared for. Her entire body felt like it might fly apart from pure nervous energy. "That's the only Sentinel you've seen? Please, tell me again."

"That is the only Sentinel we've seen," Peter said.

Hearing his voice settled Kate's nerves a little. She reached for him. "You've always been the one I can count on," she said.

Peter caught Storm's warning glance and held

her at arm's length. "Count on all of us, Kitty," he said. "We are all X-Men."

"That's not what I mean," she said. "I…"

She stopped. She'd been about to tell him about their future together: their marriage, the children they'd and lost. But she held herself back. How would Peter react? What effect would that knowledge have on him in the battle that was coming? That secret, Kate decided, was just one more part of the burden she had assumed when she had agreed to this desperate plan.

"It's all just…it's too much," she said. "I can't handle this."

"You can, and you will," Storm said. "Because you must."

"I don't know if I believe this," Wolverine said.

"Logan, you saved my life today," Kate said.

"Just doing my job, Kit."

"No, I mean in the future. We were supposed to meet because you'd gotten the last component of the device we needed to deactivate the inhibitor collars. On the way to our meeting, I had an accident, and I was attacked. You saw it happen and you saved me. It was on Park Avenue."

"You got mugged on Park Avenue?" Wolverine looked even more skeptical.

"You don't know what New York is like now. It's in ruins. There are gangs everywhere; they prey on anyone they think is a mutant, or might carry a mutant gene. They can spot us by our collars and uniforms." Reflexively Kate's hand went to her throat. "I don't have mine on."

"Kitten, listen," Storm said. "Nobody has to wear a collar."

"No, you listen. If you don't hear me, you *will* have to wear one," Kate said.

"She sure has gotten lippy just now," Wolverine said. "That's not like her. But I still don't believe it. No offense, Kit, but I think you're just scared and got your bell rung."

"Perhaps," Kurt said. "But her reaction to the Sentinel…had we even begun telling her about them? Did she even know they existed?"

Wolverine shrugged. "Ask her."

"If what she says is true, this is not thirteen-year-old Kitty."

"Now, that is an interesting question," Peter said. "Kitty. Or Kate. If you're here, what has happened to Kitty? Where is she?"

"With me, I guess. I mean, with my body," Kate said. "God, I hope she's all right. This was—is—hard enough for me. I can only imagine what it will be like for her."

"Look, whatever we're going to do about Kit-Kat, we're not gonna do it here," Logan said. "Charlie Xavier needs to know about the ambush—and he'll want to hear about the Sentinel, too. I say we get moving."

"Yes," Storm said. She put an arm around Kate's shoulders. "Keep talking, Kitten. Tell us more."

"Kate."

"All right. Kate. I'll try to remember that."

They walked quickly back to the Blackbird. Kate tried not to look at the Sentinel, and she was glad when she boarded in the plane. It wouldn't be able to see her there.

CHAPTER 4

AFTER Rachel finished the psychic projection of Kate Pryde back in time, it took less than thirty minutes for the group to shed their collars, gather anything useful they could carry in their pockets, and leave the South Bronx Mutant Internment Center—for the last time, with any luck. The Sentinels had not detected Rachel's telepathic exercise. They stood outside the fence, watching as always. But as a rule they paid little attention to what went on inside the camp, unless there was an outbreak of violence.

Rachel winced a little as they walked. The projection had left her with a fierce headache. Franklin stayed close to her. The other three—Peter, Ororo, and Magneto in his rickety wheelchair—followed in a loose group behind them, Peter carrying the unconscious Kate. He had not spoken since the projection except to whisper Kate's name every so often. Nobody had the heart to tell him to stop. "Did it work, Rach?"

"I think it did," she said. "I felt…" She glanced over her shoulder and lowered her voice. "I felt the teenage Kitty, just for a second, right at the end. Do you…I don't know what happened to her. I hope—"

"Don't," Franklin said. "This is the only thing we can do. Second-guessing will kill us."

She didn't answer. They strolled along, not hurrying, doing nothing to draw attention from the Sentinels or the other inmates—most of whom were clustered in groups for safety, around barrel fires or at the doorways of the barracks. They angled toward the perimeter fence closest to 161st Street, looking for the marker Logan was supposed to have left the night before.

"There," Ororo said quietly. All of them saw it: a newspaper box, lying on its side between the street and the sidewalk. It marked the place where, less than three feet below the asphalt surface of the former parking lot, a subway maintenance tunnel angled under the camp grounds. Storm drains just inside the fence were big enough to admit a person. The plan was simple: Logan would push one of the grates off, and they would get down into the drain as quickly as possible, then follow it to a maintenance door. That would lead to an old storage room between the storm sewers and the subway tunnel, with access to both.

From there they would head south, toward the Baxter Building, and after that...

They slowed down, to avoid being seen hanging around too close to the fence.

There was a soft scrape as the storm grate shifted and rose slowly out of its frame. Ororo looked around for the two nearest Sentinels, maybe fifty yards away on either side of the newspaper box. Neither of them appeared to have noticed.

"Let's go," she said quietly. The group picked up its collective pace, still not hurrying.

Logan's head and arms appeared as he gently set the grate down next to the open drain.

It's going to work, Rachel thought. She felt a ripple of pure elation, both at the idea of freedom and at the yearned-for possibility that she might at last have balanced the karmic scales. She couldn't bring back the mutants she had hunted down, but she could maybe do something better. She could help to undo the entire future. Her entire existing self.

She could start over again, as a girl in Xavier's school, and no commandos would ever come through the door.

With that possibility shining in her mind, she quickened her pace just a little more—and that was when Kate's eyes blinked open, and she started to scream.

"Shut her up!" Logan growled. The Sentinels at the nearest posts along the fence turned to look. Peter clapped a hand over her mouth, but Kate kept screaming into it and thrashing in his arms.

"Kate, Kate, it is all right. Peter's here."

"So are a lot of Sentinels," Rachel said. "We better move faster."

"Go," Peter said. She and Franklin ran, disappearing into the storm drain.

All of the Sentinels were on full alert now, and once they powered up their repulsors they would lay down a devastating concentration of fire. The X-Men had to get out before that happened.

The impact of an energy beam blasted a large, irregular crater in the asphalt between Peter and the drain. He stumbled and put a hand out to break his fall, inadvertently uncovering Kate's mouth.

"Peter! Peter, what happened to you? Where are we?! What's going on?" Twisting around, Kate saw Ororo and cried out again. "Ororo! What's happening?"

"Mutants, any attempt to escape will be cause for termination," one of the Sentinels said from the fence line, less than thirty yards away. Storm whirled and raised her arms, summoning lightning that seemed to come from every part of the sky at once. It crackled along the entire length of the fence, blasting into every Sentinel patrolling there. They were staggered, but the backup Sentinels coming from within the camp were not.

Another Sentinel's beam thrummed past Peter, who transformed into his steel form and threw the first piece of broken concrete he found back at the robot. The concrete crashed into it, shattering the lens on its torso repulsor. The other Sentinels sidestepped as it stumbled, clearing their field of fire.

Peter hurled more pieces of rock and debris at the approaching Sentinels, trying to buy Magnus some time while carrying Kate toward the drain. The broken ground was difficult for Magnus' wheelchair. While the Sentinels at the fence were still recovering, the ones inside the compound would make short work of him. One of them stomped straight through a nearby barracks from its post deeper in the camp. Others were coming from the headquarters just inside the front gate. Soon they would have the mutants trapped in the open space between the fence and the barracks.

"The mutants are not wearing inhibitor collars," one of the Sentinels boomed. Others relayed the message up and down the fence.

"Peter, put me down, please, please, put me down!"

He knelt and turned his broad back to the oncoming Sentinel, shielding the woman he loved from anything they might fire or throw. "Kate," he said. "Are you back already? Did it work? What did Xavier say?"

"What are you talking about?" She looked around wildly. "Where are we? Back from what? Peter, what's going on? And nobody's ever called me Kate in my life. What's happening?!"

It hit him then. Rachel had not just projected Kate's psyche back into Kitty. She had *switched* the two of them in each other's bodies—or more correctly, into the temporally distant versions of their own bodies.

"Peter!" Storm shouted from the edge of the drain. "Is she awake? Get her in here!"

A blast from another Sentinel repulsor hit Peter a glancing blow. His organic-steel body absorbed and dissipated the heat, but the impact knocked him forward. He held Kate with one arm and punched the other one forearm-deep into the melted asphalt, stopping himself. Letting her go, he pulled himself free and said, "Okay, my love. Run."

Something strange happened to her face when he said *my love*. If they hadn't been in the middle of a combined jailbreak and battle for the lives of the entire human race, Peter might well have died of embarrassment. Of course she couldn't know they were married. And what must he have sounded like, saying that to a girl of thirteen?

"The guy in the wheelchair, he's getting stuck!" she cried out. Then she said incredulously, "Is that *Magneto?*"

"Yes," Peter said. "We have few allies now, and need all we have."

"You need him? For what?"

"Are you looking around you, girl?" he shouted at her. "There are maybe ten living mutants on this continent, and we are all about to be killed by Sentinels. Having Magneto on our side is not the oddest thing you will see tonight…if we live to see the rest of tonight!"

He immediately felt miserable for yelling at her.

Peter took two giant steps toward the drain. Storm had already gone through it, down and away. Peter, Kate, and Magneto were the last three. Getting through would be impossible in his steel form; he would have to transform back just as he approached, and hope the Sentinels didn't pick him off in the moment between his transformation and his disappearance into the haven of New York's stormwater drainage system.

"Kate! Kitty, whichever! Let's go!" he cried out. But when he looked back, not only was she not following him, she was going back for Magneto.

THE DAMNED chair would be the death of him. He supposed it was only just that he should die in a wheelchair, having been responsible for Charles dying in one. Karma, some might call it. Or poetic justice. What Magneto called it was death. And although he was more than one hundred years old and had lost the use of his legs, he had no interest whatsoever in experiencing death.

It looked, however, as if the choice would not be left up to him.

He forced the chair foot by foot over the ground. The pavement was pitted by years of neglect and thousands of Sentinel footfalls, and Magneto had never possessed Colossus's enormous physical strength. There were four Sentinels within striking distance; although Ororo had disabled a number of the others with her lightning strike, those four would be more than enough to eliminate him.

Something tickled at the back of his mind—an idea that would not quite form, and probably would never have the chance, given the circumstances.

"Magneto!" Kate called. Something about her diction had changed, her posture…and then he knew. Rachel, thought Magneto, you have outdone yourself.

He pushed himself harder and shouted at her. "Stupid girl! Go!"

She was less than twenty feet away now. Behind her, Colossus had turned around, as well, and was returning for him. "Piotr, I forbid this!" he shouted. "You must survive! Get out of here!"

Colossus ignored him, and a moment later the world around all three of them disappeared in thunder and fire.

IN THE stormwater tunnel, the impact knocked everyone off their feet. The sound seemed to take forever to echo away down the maze of passages, and the water in the tunnel's central trench rippled and sloshed back and forth from the impact above.

Wolverine was the first to call out. "Everyone sound off."

"I'm here," Rachel said. "And Franklin's right next to me."

"'Ro? You in here?"

"Yes."

Franklin switched on a flashlight, their only one, and played the beam around the tunnel until he saw her. She was closest to the   vertical drain shaft and had taken the worst of the explosion. Blood ran in her hair and down one leg.

"Where's Kate and Peter?"

"They went back for Magneto," Ororo said. "They're still up there. So is he." She felt heavy with the knowledge that already they might have lost half their team. No, not they: she. Leadership had always been difficult for Ororo, because she felt the responsibility for those she commanded more personally than was healthy.

"Well, there's no going back for 'em now," Logan said. "We have to move. Nobody use powers. They need to think we're dead, or else we're not getting anywhere."

"Wait, wait!" Rachel said. She caught

Franklin's arm and aimed the flashlight at the collapsed part of the tunnel, where rubble nearly choked it off. Beyond that, to the south, was the route to freedom. "Look," Rachel said. The rest of them saw a steel elbow and forearm, a flash of red.

"Let's get digging." Wolverine started probing at the rubble. Above and around them, the steel reinforcing the tunnel groaned and shifted. "And let's do it fast. This isn't going to hold forever."

"Especially if Sentinels start stomping around up there," Rachel said.

"He must be out cold, or he'd be digging himself out," Logan said.

"But he's not dead, or he'd revert to human form. So let's get it done." Franklin stepped to Logan's side; the two of them started shifting rubble, as carefully and quickly as they could. Rachel pitched in, too. When they uncovered Peter's head, she held it and started talking to him, trying to wake him up.

Ororo came to help, as well, but Logan held

her back. "Take a minute, 'Ro. You need it. We got this."

So she sat, and watched, and waited for her hearing to come all the way back. She wondered what had become of Magneto and Kate Pryde. So much death already, Ororo thought. Did they really have any chance?

MAGNETO slowly recovered his senses. He smelled burning hair, and he tried to get up and run before he remembered that he had lost the use of his legs, long ago, in a situation not unlike this one. He raised his head and saw a smoking crater, filled with debris, where the stormwater drain had been. That avenue of escape, it seemed, had been cut off permanently. The Sentinels were calling out warnings, but he couldn't hear them very well with the explosion still ringing in his ears. Of Peter and Kate there was no sign.

The others…he could not keep in his mind who the others had been. He knew he was suffering some kind of blast injury because there was an idea dancing just at the edge of his cognition. But he was an old man, and he could not bring it into focus.

He began to drag himself away from the edge of the crater, looking through the smoke for his wheelchair. He spotted it, farther down along the crater's edge toward the fence. A Sentinel stood there, watching him. Then it shifted its gaze.

Propping himself on one elbow, Magneto turned to see what it was looking at. Kate Pryde stood unscathed at the edge of the crater, having instinctively phased when her body felt the first whisper of overpressure in the air.

"Go, girl," he said.

"How? The hole—"

"Phase, dammit. You just did, at the explosion. How do you think you're still alive? Now do it again! Go! Now!"

She looked over his shoulder, apparently at another Sentinel, because her eyes grew very wide and her form translucent. Then she dropped straight down into the ground and was gone.

He was trapped, by himself in the camp, with Sentinels all around.

But as he had said to the group just an hour or so before: Max Eisenhardt had spent part of his childhood in a camp not unlike this one. Magneto would not end his days here.

"Mutant 067, do not move!" the nearest Sentinel commanded. "Your next potentially hostile action will result in immediate termination."

All actions are potentially hostile, Magneto thought. It was a critical flaw in the Sentinels' approach that they did not understand that.

Then something dawned on him, the idea he had not been able to catch a moment before. His head was beginning to clear. It was time to take his own advice, was it not? He had fought the Nazis. He had fought the X-Men. He had fought Hydra, and the first generations of Sentinels, and more other enemies than he could enumerate. And then, for almost twenty years, he had been a prisoner. Confined to a wheelchair, a collar on his neck for so long that he had nearly forgotten he had any powers to inhibit.

Powers like the ones Kitty had just exhibited. Colossus, as well. He wondered briefly whether Kate Pryde would be having the same difficulty back in the past...if, indeed, she had survived the projection.

"Godspeed, friends," Magneto said softly.

He felt the lines and fields of magnetic force around him. And for the first time in more than fifteen years, he began to focus, their patterns and idiosyncrasies flooding back into his consciousness. The rush of it blasted through his endocrine system and into his mind, filling him with a joy he had forgotten how to feel. For a moment, he almost believed that he could walk again, so powerful was the surge. Then he refocused his attention and began to concentrate his power on his chair.

"Exercise of your powers will result in immediate termination," the Sentinel warned.

"I'm only getting my wheelchair, Sentinel," Magneto said in his best old-man quaver.

The Sentinel hesitated, for the briefest moment. But that was all Magneto needed to see the fields and currents of magnetism inside its body. With the slightest mental tug, he tore it apart.

CHAPTER 5

ON THE Blackbird, Storm continued trying to probe at Kate's story. "Tell me again," she said. "How were you going to get free of the collars so Rachel could send you back?"

"Logan did most of the work," Kate said. "He spends a lot of time in Canada, with the Free Canadian Army. There are rumors that some other mutants are up there, too, but we don't know for sure. They put together a jamming device that masked the fields from the inhibitor collars so we could remove them. Then we could use our powers—but we didn't know how long it would last. Once they sent me back, the rest of the group was going to break out of the camp and head for the Baxter Building."

"The Baxter Building?"

"That's the Sentinels' command center. We

needed to disable them, their whole operation. If we didn't, things were going to get a lot worse."

"From what you have already told us, that does not seem possible," Peter said.

"But it is," Kate said. "The Sentinels are planning to expand their anti-mutant operations to other continents once they've completely pacified North America. Europe has been watching, and they've seen how the Sentinels work. They just slaughter everyone they think might be a threat, and only leave enough alive to do research so they can do a better job of killing next time. So the Europeans have decided there's only one thing they can do. Tomorrow, they're going to nuke every Sentinel installation they can find."

"Good riddance," Logan said from the cockpit, where he was finishing preflight checks while the Blackbird's engines warmed up.

"One of those installations is in the Baxter Building," Kate said. "There are others in cities all over North America. Hundreds of them. It's not going to be a surgical strike. It's going to be a nuclear apocalypse."

There was a brief silence while they all digested this. "Well, that's a little different," Logan said. "If it's true."

He backed the Blackbird around, then waited while Max-X guards cleared the bodies of Hellfire Club mercenaries from the landing strip. One of the guards waved an all-clear. Logan eased the Blackbird forward through a tight turn, aiming it back up the runway just north of the prison. "Windy as hell," he grumbled. "Hate taking off in this."

As the Blackbird picked up speed, everyone strapped in to a semicircle of seats at the front end of the passenger cabin. Farther back was a narrow passage between compartments jammed with surveillance equipment and other stores, making the Blackbird a mobile command center.

Logan glared at the Sentinel, still standing watch as the Max-X staff got on with their cleanup.

Coming over the spine of the Rockies, Kate saw a formation of cargo helicopters. Support crews and equipment, probably, she thought. It was going to be a while before Max-X was a suitable place to imprison anyone more dangerous than a car thief.

Looking at the Sentinel, she had a shiver of recollection, picturing the pickets of Sentinels around the perimeter of the camp in the South Bronx.

"Wish we had onboard missiles," Logan said. "It'd do me good to slag that tin can on our way out."

"That's going to be part of our debrief with Professor Xavier," Ororo said. "A s well as the Hellfire Club ambush. You know they were after you, Kitten, don't you?"

Kate hadn't given it a thought. "They were? I mean, I just woke up in the middle of everything. Yes, I remember a long time ago they… what did they want me for?"

"It doesn't matter now," Peter said. "That's over. Let us not confuse her, Ororo. She is having a difficult time, whatever the reason."

"Also I think we should be more concerned with the Brotherhood than with the Hellfire Club," Nightcrawler said.

"You got that right, Kurt," Logan called over the rising roar of the Blackbird's engines. "I think the whole time-travel thing is a smoke screen. I don't doubt for a second the Brotherhood's behind this."

Kate didn't know how to answer this. It seemed cruel that Logan was the fulcrum of all their plans in the future, yet here he dismissed her story out of hand.

The Blackbird picked up speed and lifted off, skimming over the foothills and climbing sharply to reach cruising altitude. The Rocky Mountains fell behind and the high plains appeared, stretching unbroken to the horizon. Logan leveled off at fifty thousand feet, well above commercial traffic, and pointed the Blackbird east-northeast.

Kate stayed quiet as long as she could,

needing the time to collect herself and knowing that she was asking her friends to believe a story that seemed crazy from beginning to end—or perhaps from end to beginning, since they were now in a time period before her actual story began. But soon she started to feel that the longer she let the silence go, the more likely it became that the rest of the X-Men would find ways to dismiss her. If that happened, she would be stuck here, or put in a padded room somewhere in Xavier's mansion while they worked on her mind. Meanwhile, the future versions of these people who had become so dear to her would die.

Perhaps her own future self would die...or was already dead? If so, what would happen to wide-eyed Kitty, the newly minted X-Man with no idea of what her future held? Would she be returned to her body if Kate's was killed in the future? Or would Kitty's mind dissipate into the psychic ether, leaving Kate to relive, Cassandra-like, the coming terrible years?

Fear got her talking again, and she knew she

sounded scared. "Logan, I thought at least you would believe me."

"Me? What the hell gave you that idea?"

"Two or three hours ago you saved my life. I guess that's what."

"Hell of a story, Kit-Kat. But it just doesn't hang together." Logan engaged the Blackbird's autopilot and turned around in the pilot's chair. "Everybody hear me out. The Blob was one of the original Brotherhood members, right? We know that."

"Yes," Ororo said.

"And he's such a wad that nobody except the Brotherhood would lift a finger to help him, right?"

"Okay."

"So today he breaks out of Max-X, and Kit has this episode not two hours later."

"*Genau*," Nightcrawler jumped in. "And now she is warning us about the Brotherhood. Do you believe in that kind of coincidence?"

Logan was shaking his head. "I don't believe in any kind of coincidence. But we don't have to believe her to know something shifty's going on. Try this one: Emma Frost or some other mind-control mastermind—hell, maybe Mastermind himself—is doing this to get us all ruffled and sucker us all into being there for a big attack on not just Xavier, but all the X-Men they can get."

"Now that is a conspiracy theory," Peter commented.

"You're damn right it is, Petey, because one way or another we're dealing with a conspiracy. I just don't think it has anything to do with time travel."

"You're wrong," Kate said. "Listen to you making up a story, just because you don't like the one *I'm* telling."

"The story I'm making up doesn't involve time travel and mutant concentration camps," Logan said. "You tell me, Kit. Would you believe you, if you were hearing this story?"

"How about we all cool off?" Ororo said. "Kitty's story is difficult to believe, but it will be easy enough to disprove. We'll be in Washington,

D.C., in about an hour. Then we will touch base with Professor Xavier and see what he can sense inside Kitty's mind."

"Seems like maybe we ought to just give him a call," Wolverine said. "Save ourselves the detour. The kid needs help."

"As you said, Logan, this may be a mind-control initiative by Emma Frost or a Brother-hood telepath," Storm said. "Taking that into ac-count, we must also consider the possibility that any communication channel is compromised. The only thing we can do is get to Washington and speak to Xavier directly. He will need to be in close contact with Kitty—or Kate—to un-derstand what has happened to her mind in any case. No point in agitating him before he can take any real action."

"Okay, 'Ro. If you say so. I'm just the chauf-feur." Logan visibly checked out of the conver-sation, focusing on piloting the Blackbird. They were already over the plains of the Oklahoma Panhandle, and Logan banked the Blackbird slightly north to skip around a thunderstorm visible ahead.

Storm thought for a moment, and then turned to Kate. "You said Logan saved your life. What were you doing out of the camp?"

"I'm kind of a trustee there," Kate said. "They send me—the Sentinels, I mean—they send me on errands sometimes. Most of the non-mutant inmates in the camp are just criminals. So the Sentinels use us as couriers. They make sure we know that if anything goes wrong, the other mutants will suffer for it. Just this morning I was taking tissue samples to a lab at Hunter College. Or what used to be Hunter College. Now it's just a research lab."

Kate was still getting used to the sound of her adolescent voice, the astonishing energy and restlessness of being a teenager. Even her teeth felt different. Another wave of shock and unease swept over her. It didn't help that she kept looking at Peter, who had no idea what their future held. He was leaning into the Blackbird's small medical bay, getting some kind of field treatment for the wound in his shoulder. It wouldn't slow him down much when he was in his steel form, but even a slight disability could be a problem if they were going to be taking on the Brotherhood.

"Kitty," Storm prompted. "I mean Kate. Go on, please."

She looked away from Peter. "I…tripped, I guess. Or there was some kind of trap set in the sidewalk. But I fell through and there were Rogues there."

"But you got here. Logan saved you from these Rogues, and…?"

"Rachel thought up a plan to…project my mind back into me here," Kate said. "This earlier me, I mean."

"You've had quite a shock, Kitty," Ororo said. "Take it slow. We would like to believe you, but—"

"Funny you should say that," Kate said. "I remember you telling me the hardest part of this operation would be convincing you of the truth."

"Touché," Nightcrawler said. "Listen to her, Ororo. Look at her. Does she speak and move like a girl of thirteen?"

"No, she doesn't," Ororo admitted.

"Well, she wouldn't, if an adult woman was pulling her strings," Logan said. "What we oughta do is head for home and get our little Kitten to a real doctor—"

"Don't talk to me like I'm a girl," Kate said. "I'm thirty-five years old. And if you don't listen to me, there's…" She was at a loss, trying to describe everything that lay in their future. "You have to listen to me. If they kill Senator Kelly, Professor Xavier's going to be next. And there won't be any stopping it."

"It seems to me that the safe thing would be to touch base with Professor Xavier," Peter said. "He will be able to see what is happening inside our Kitty's mind. Then, if necessary, it's a short trip from Washington, D.C., to home."

"Waste of time," Logan said. "If she's inventing kids for Scott—"

"I'm not," Kate said. "I had children, too." Her eyes looked off into the distance. "We would have had more, even as bad as things were getting, but mutants are forbidden to breed—"

"Kitty," Storm said. "Let's get back on track. If you want us to believe you, we need you to be very specific about how this happened and what you think we should do."

"And let's not forget, she's got us all palling around with Magneto, too," Logan said.

"That's enough, Logan. You're making things worse."

"You got it, 'Ro. Lip zipped. You have fun with story time."

As far as any of them knew, Magneto was dead following a confrontation with the X-Men in the Savage Land, when his polar fortress collapsed. If he was alive—which, given his resilience, was certainly possible—he had been keeping a low profile. It seemed fantastic that he would reconcile with the X-Men in the way Kate's story suggested. "Are you sure about Magneto?" Ororo asked.

"Right before I left, he said something about living in a concentration camp when he was a child, and not wanting to die in one. That's the last thing I remember about him. And he's in a wheelchair. The Sentinels paralyzed him when they attacked a base of his in the Caribbean. I think he said it was right after the Mutant Control Act was passed."

"Mutant Control Act. I do not like the sound of that," Nightcrawler said. He would be one of the first to be controlled, due to his unusual appearance, and he knew it. "When was this act passed? Or should I say when will it be?"

"Five years from now," Kate said. "After Kelly's assassination and the next election. Things get worse fast." She looked toward the cockpit. "Of all of us, only Logan is free, in my time. He's the one who got us the parts for the Jammer."

"That got you out of your collars," Ororo prompted.

"Right. Then we were ready. Rachel…did whatever she did, and then the rest were going to break out of the camp, with Logan's help."

"This is getting us back to the nuclear attack from Europe?"

Kate nodded. "Yes, the only chance we have...had? I don't even know how to talk about this. The only chance was to take out the Sentinels at their command center, cripple their communications so the Europeans would hold off on their attack. We were all...I don't know, going to go to Canada or something. If it worked."

It occurred to her that the events she was describing were, in a sense, happening even as she spoke. If time moved the same way, at the same speed...if any of it was real... "They might already all be dead," she said. "I might be. If my body is dead there—"

"Try not to think about it," Ororo said. "Nobody's unlocked the puzzle of time yet, and we will not be the first. What we need to know is what we tell Professor Xavier if we're going to pull him out of a Senate hearing."

"Tell him he's going to die," Kate said. "Tell

him if the Brotherhood assassinates Senator Kelly, we're all going to die."

There was silence in the Blackbird. Then Kate said, "I can't believe I made it. Rachel said she could do it, but I didn't believe her. She… I guess I owe her an apology, if I ever see her again. If…I wonder where the teenage me is."

"She's fine," Ororo said. "You have to believe that. This is against my better judgment, but I think I believe you, Kate Pryde. And if what you're saying is true, we need you absolutely focused and committed, if we are going to avert this future."

Nightcrawler spoke up again. "I am dead, as well, *nicht wahr,* Kitten?"

"A long time ago," she said.

"A long time ago, and not so very far in the future," Kurt mused. "No one really understands time, I suppose."

"Here's a time we can understand. We're going to be in D.C. in about forty minutes," Logan said. "All we can do until then is hang tight."

CHAPTER 6

KITTY stopped shaking about the time Wolverine finished digging Colossus out of the rubble from the tunnel collapse. The job should have gone quicker, but Rachel couldn't use her telekinetic abilities for fear of drawing the Sentinels to them.

Kitty couldn't do anything but look around her and tremble. She was old. Look how old she was. She tried to talk, then shied away from the sound of her own voice. The others...all of them except Logan were so much older. "What's happening?" she asked, over and over.

Ororo came over to her. Logan was busy digging, Peter was buried, and the other two watched the collapsed area for some sign of... "Was that Magneto?" Kitty asked incredulously.

"It was," Ororo said.

"You guys are friends with *Magneto*?"

She'd sunk through the tunnel ceiling just as the X-Men freed themselves from the falling debris and figured out that Colossus was trapped. Kitty was on a thin edge, with different kinds of madness on either side.

The X-Men, with the exception of Peter, were equally confused. Peter was still being excavated from under a hundred tons of rock and steel, so he wasn't contributing to the conversation. The others spoke quietly, knowing the Sentinels would be searching. As long as they stayed underground, they would probably be safe. The Sentinels were too big to operate effectively in the tunnels.

"So, did it work?" asked a man Kitty didn't recognize. He'd stuck close to the red-haired woman. "Who did you see?"

"See?" Kitty had no idea what he was talking about. "Who was I supposed to see?"

Logan pulled Peter free of the rubble. Peter muttered in Russian. One of his eyelids wouldn't stop twitching.

"Hold off with the questions, Franklin,"

Ororo said. "There's something going on here. Kate—"

"You're all so *old*," Kitty said in wonder, looking at Peter and then Ororo. "And I don't even know you," she said to Franklin. "Or you," to Rachel.

"What are you talking about, Kate?" Franklin asked. "Of course you know us. Did you hit your head? How old do you think you are?"

"Thirteen," she said. "I won't be fourteen for another couple of months."

"Oh, my God," Rachel said. "It worked. The switch worked."

Kitty's mouth opened, closed, opened again. "Switch? You switched me with my old self?"

"We're not that old, Kitten," Ororo said.

Kitty wondered whether Ororo had looked in a mirror lately. "You were just...I just saw you a minute ago! And you were..." She stalled, too many questions competing for space in her brain. "You switched me? Why? What...what is this place?"

"New York. South Bronx," Logan said.

"But…the Sentinels? And who's…is the Kitty from now back in my body?"

"We call her Kate, but yes," Ororo said.

Kitty paused for a long moment. Then she said, with a brittle laugh, "Boy, they told me I'd see some strange stuff in the X-Men. Where's everyone else? Angel, Nightcrawler?"

Now it was Logan and Ororo's turn to pause. Rachel and Franklin looked to them, since they'd been there when this teenage Kitty had joined the X-Men.

"Kit-Kat," Logan said, "I'm going to hit you with it all at once. Everyone you don't see right here is dead, except for a couple of guys in Alpha Flight, and I'm not sure about them. We're about to raid the Sentinel HQ in the Baxter Building. If we don't take it out, there's going to be a nuclear strike and all of us will be dead." He looked her in the eye, keeping her gaze focused on his. "Those are the facts. We sent Kate back in time to see if we could do something about it, and you showed up here. Guess your mind needed a place to hang out while future-you checked out your time again."

"I time-traveled and body-switched, all at once," Kitty said. Her voice was almost entirely drained of inflection. "And Peter said *my love*—"

"We'll talk about that later," Ororo said.

Kitty looked at Peter, who was studying the ground. The whole situation was too many kinds of wrong. She opened her mouth and started talking, trying to anchor herself with the sound of her own voice. "I can't handle this. I can't handle this. I can't handle this!"

"Kit-Kat, you need to handle it, because we need you," Logan said. "Now let's get moving. First person makes a *Freaky Friday* joke gets claws in his gizzard."

THEY moved fast through the abandoned maintenance tunnel, angling back into the main tunnel that crossed under the Harlem River into Manhattan. "Only a hundred and some blocks to the Baxter Building," Logan said. "We take this tunnel straight down to Grand Central, come up on 42nd Street, we're right there. Piece of cake, unless we run into a collapse."

"Or Rogues," the red-haired woman said. Her name was Rachel, but that was all Kitty knew about her.

"Mind-control 'em. Set 'em on each other and watch the fun," Logan said. "Easy, right?"

"Sure, easy," Rachel said. "Until it brings the Sentinels down on us."

"That's gonna happen anyway, Rachel. Sooner or later they're gonna know where we are. All that means is we gotta be ready to fight. Kitten, how you doing?"

"I'm having a little trouble, Logan. I mean…a lot of trouble. My body doesn't feel right. My eyes are different, I'm…bigger all over, my voice…this doesn't even feel like me! And everyone's dead, and—"

Abruptly she stopped talking—so abruptly that Ororo shot a warning glance at Rachel, who shook her head. "I didn't do anything," Rachel said.

"I'm okay," Kitty said. "I'll get a grip, I'll handle it. But did we have to leave Magneto? I always thought of him as an enemy, but seeing him in his wheelchair…it reminded me of Professor Xavier."

"The Sentinels almost collapsed the tunnel on us, Kitten," Ororo said. "There was no way for us to get back and help him." Sadly she added, "When I think of what he said, about not ending his days in such a place…it's cruel, what happened to him."

"I'll bet he gave 'em hell before they got him, though. Ol' Magnus wasn't going to screw around once his collar was off," Logan said.

"A noble death is still a death," Peter said. "I am sick of death."

"We don't know for sure he's dead," Kitty said. "I don't believe it."

A BOOM echoed up and down the tunnel as they

approached the 96th Street station. It was empty and dark. The ticket booth's bulletproof glass was shattered, and its contents—including several bones—had been scattered around the turnstiles.

"What's that?" Franklin said. Another boom shook the tunnel. Pieces of concrete, from pebbles to blocks the size of a human being, fell onto the platform and the tracks.

Then, with a deafening sound of rending metal and collapsing concrete, the station ceiling was torn away, revealing the night sky—and three Sentinels looming through the hole.

"Sentinels!" Franklin cried out reflexively. The air shifted as he began to focus his powers, but a blinding energy beam as wide as Colossus' shoulder lanced down through the hole and incinerated Franklin where he stood.

The blast of the beam's impact on the tunnel floor drowned out Rachel's screams and knocked all of them sprawling. Ororo hit the tracks, her senses dulled by the sound and smoke. Her mind spun back to a conversation a few weeks before. They'd just confirmed that Logan could get them the Jammer. Briefly intoxicated with the glimmer of possibility, Kate had said: *We should get the collars off and show them what we can do. Franklin could just* think *the Baxter Building out of existence.*

I…no, Franklin had said. *No. I can't do that kind of reality-shifting anymore. The consequences…I can't control them.*

Rachel had tried to convince him, but even she could not break through the psychological barrier—or get him to explain his reasoning any further. *No,* Franklin had said over and over. *I can't.*

Perhaps he had been correct to worry. Once a mutant of Franklin's power started tinkering with the fabric of reality, there was no way to know for certain where the ramifications of that change would stop.

Now it no longer mattered.

As they scrambled to their feet, the Sentinels broadcast an alert. "Patrol 3L-40 has contacted mutant escapees. All patrols respond."

The other Sentinels' torso-embedded repulsors were charging. "Surrender or face immediate termination," one of the Sentinels said. "You will receive no other warning."

All of them froze for a moment, conditioned by years of prison and inhibitor collars to obey Sentinel commands. "You call that a warning?" Logan growled.

Rachel, with a howl of agonized fury, unleashed a telekinetic pulse that turned the molecules of the atmosphere itself into a blast wave. It struck the Sentinel that had killed Franklin with the equivalent of the overpressure from a megaton nuclear bomb. The Sentinel's head and torso disintegrated into shrapnel, peppering the two on either side of it, staggering but not damaging them.

"Control," one of the Sentinels said. "Escapees also not wearing inhibitor—ZZZKK!"

Storm shot up out of the subway station, unleashing a blast of lightning that interrupted the Sentinel's transmission. Electricity arced between the two Sentinels, momentarily causing the lights of nearby traffic signals to blink. Then they went dark again, and the Sentinels regained their balance. Their repulsors began to charge again, the process reset by the electrical interference.

Storm hit both of them with another blast, but their insulation and composite structure lessened the lightning's effect. She was damaging them, but not fast enough.

Down in the tunnel, Colossus gleamed in the lightning flashes, his banded organic-steel body tensing to join the battle. Kate ducked away from him, under the remaining roof overhang, searching for a way to help. Logan saw Colossus and yelled out, "How long's it been, Petey?!"

"Far too long, Wolverine!"

Logan jumped toward Colossus, who caught him and launched him upward in the first Fastball Special seen for almost twenty years. The *snikt* of Wolverine's claws cut through the din of the battle just as the Adamantium slashed through the side of the Sentinel's face, gouging out one of its eyes and exposing interior circuitry for a follow-up slash as Logan landed on its shoulder. A high electronic squeal, uncomfortably like a scream, burst from two different places in the Sentinel's cranial assembly.

It clapped a huge hand onto its shoulder, smashing Logan down and grabbing him up in its fist. "TerminationSQUEEEEEE," it said, the voice coming from the hole in its head as well as its mouth. The sound would have burst a normal man's eardrums, and the pressure of its fist was slowly crushing even Logan's Adamantium-reinforced body.

"Storm! You got an opening here!" he yelled. "Finish this sucker!"

Lightning split the sky, hitting the Sentinel squarely in the head. Its fist spasmed open as the electrical charge coursed through it—and through Logan, who fell, stunned, to crash down on the roof of a long-abandoned car.

Rachel and Colossus were coming out of the station onto the street. Rachel knocked the

remaining Sentinel spinning with another telekinetic blast, and Storm summoned lightning
that crackled around her body as she hung fifty
feet in the air. But Storm couldn't release the
charge—Rachel was too close to the Sentinel
and too far gone in her berserk grief to listen.

As Storm waited for her chance, she spotted three more Sentinels, coming at a run down
Lexington from the north. Their footsteps shook
loose bricks and shards of glass from the abandoned buildings on either side of the street.

Colossus saw them, too. Four at once? he
thought. They could not fight so many, or the
others that were surely coming, unless they kept
moving. Guerrilla tactics: hit and run.

As all four Sentinels passed in front of a
derelict hotel, Colossus put his head down and
built up a head of steam. He drove himself into
the corner of the building and along the length
of its front wall, smashing the support beams as
he went. The building sagged into an avalanche
of bricks and steel, burying the Sentinels in six

stories of rubble and collapsing another part of the damaged subway station across the street.

"Yeah!" Wolverine shouted. "Attaboy, Petey!"

Colossus turned back to rejoin the group. He clambered over the rubble, seeing the remains of one Sentinel partially exposed. Its eyes were blank, and he felt a pang of conscience at what he had done. This was his curse, to be a peaceful man gifted with powers that made him indispensable in a time of war.

Scared out of hiding by the rain of concrete and steel inside the station, Kitty Pryde reached street level just in time to see the wreckage shift under Colossus. An armored purple arm reached up and out, grabbing his leg and pulling him down. The rest of the Sentinel slowly appeared, wreckage cascading around its damaged, sparking body. It raised Colossus up. He twisted and turned in its grip. But dangling as he was from one foot, he couldn't get the leverage to pry its fingers loose.

"Kate!" Logan shouted. He ran toward the

Sentinel and jumped, using his claws like ice axes to climb its body. "Do the phasing thing!"

"What? Why?" she asked.

Logan started hacking at the Sentinel's arm. It snapped the arm back, sending Logan flying over Kitty's head into what had once been a restaurant storefront. The Sentinel was broadcasting a request for reinforcements at deafening volume, periodically interrupted by gibberish and electronic noise.

"Just do it!" Logan shouted from inside the restaurant. He was struggling to get loose from the pile of tables and chairs his impact had shaken up.

Kitty covered the distance to the Sentinel in ten steps and reached out, feeling herself become incorporeal as her fingertips touched its leg. She passed through it and felt energy surge all around without touching her. There was a sound, a high-pitched mechanical scream. When she passed out the other side of the Sentinel, a rain of sparks was falling around her and Colossus was landing flat on his back on the street.

Kitty looked up as the Sentinel's enormous bulk sagged down toward her, smoke leaking from its joints and eyes. She phased again, feeling it pass through her to sprawl face-down on the edge of the debris mountain left by the hotel's collapse. When she was clear of it again, she became solid and smelled burned circuitry and insulation.

"I forgot, you haven't learned that yet," Logan said, wiping machine oils and hydraulic fluids off his claws with a tablecloth. "When you phase through something that's got electrical works, your phasing fries them—for a minute, at least."

"Good to know," Kitty said. She looked at the fallen Sentinel and thought: I did that. A fierce pride rose in her. She was part of the X-Men. They were going to save the world.

"Company is coming, friends," Colossus said. "We were not subtle."

"Then let's get outta here," Logan said. "Back into the tunnels."

"That restricts our movement," Ororo objected.

"I got a plan, 'Ro. Remember, I've had a lot of time to set things up out here, and I couldn't tell you everything while you were in Camp Sunshine up in the Bronx. Okay?"

Looking both curious and irritated, Ororo said, "Yes. Okay. But you will tell us very soon, Logan. No secrets."

"You got it, babe. Let's move."

Rachel was first back down into the station. She paused, gazing at the spot where she had lost her husband. The rest of the X-Men gathered around her, knowing Sentinel reinforcements were near. They only had a moment, perhaps, but they owed Franklin a moment.

Where he had been, the tunnel floor was blackened, the tracks melted into a puddle that had yet to solidify. The nearest part of the concrete platform had been vaporized in a neat arc. Of Franklin himself there was only ash.

Rachel wept at the sight. "When he died,"

she sobbed. "Storm, I felt it! He was in my mind, and then—"

"I know, Rachel," Ororo said. "But we need you. We need you now. You must save your grief, or his death will have been wasted."

"I don't want to hear about wasted deaths, or noble deaths, or sacrifices! No more death!" Rachel screamed. "It's too much…"

Logan spun her around and leaned in close, holding her by both arms. "Rach, I'm not gonna tell you how to feel. And I'm not gonna tell you what to do. But I am gonna tell you that if we don't get moving, we're gonna be looking at thirty Sentinels instead of three. What do you think will happen then?"

"Maybe I don't care," she said.

"Okay. You stay here, then. Hell, all of you can stay here. Then the Sentinels will have it nice and easy. But me, I'm not done killing yet. See you later." Logan turned and started walking south, dropping down to the tunnel floor when he reached the end of the platform.

"Rachel," Ororo said. "Logan's not gentle, but he is correct."

Rachel knelt at the edge of the scorched area and ran her finger along the end of one of the tracks, looking thoughtfully at the soot her fingertip picked up. She rubbed it onto her other fingers and stood back up.

"Goodbye, Franklin," she said, and turned to follow Logan south into the darkness.

WHAT we're gonna do once we get to Grand Central is skip over into the old Metro-North tunnels," Wolverine said as they passed through the 51st Street station. "We can't stay together. Two groups: me and Petey in one, and Kitty, Rachel and Ororo in the other."

"And how will we communicate?" Peter asked. "Rachel can reach out to us telepathically, but the Sentinels will locate her if she does."

"I know," Logan said. "That's where my compadres in the FCA come in."

"They are here? The Free Canadian Army

is in New York?" Ororo asked.

"'Roro, you know I like to work alone. But even I'm not enough of a lone wolf to take on every Sentinel in New York with just the five of us. You'll see how it works in a minute."

It was actually closer to twenty minutes by the time they reached a branch in the tunnel that connected them to the Metro-North network. A voice came from the darkness. "What's the password?"

"Nobody told me the goddamn password, Rick," Logan said. "But I can smell you, and you know my voice. So put your gun down and let's get this show on the road."

A light came on a few yards away, illuminating an old train car with a cluster of a dozen or so armed men and women near its middle door. "Free Canadian Army, meet the X-Men," Logan said. "X-Men, FCA."

The closest of the FCA soldiers stepped up to tap fists with Logan. "Thought there were going to be six of you?"

"Should have been seven. We got one extra because Kate here woke up, only she's actually her thirteen-year-old self. Long story. But we also lost two. Franklin bought it on the way down, and the old man didn't make it out of the camp."

Rick nodded. "That change anything?"

"Nope," Logan said. "We still need you to keep an eye on the Sentinels and get us close to the Baxter Building. You up for it?"

"Hey, we didn't come all the way down from Sault Ste. Marie just to see a show," one of the other FCA soldiers said.

"Oh, you will see a show, all right," Storm said.

"Are we sure that Magneto didn't make it out of the camp?" Kitty asked. "I heard one of the Sentinels say something about us also not having inhibitor collars on.'"

"I heard that, too," Peter said. "But we cannot be sure of the Sentinel's syntax. It could have meant that we as well as Magneto had no collars. Or it could have meant that in addition to escaping, we also had no collars."

"But Magneto *didn't* have his collar on. Rachel, can you—?"

"No. Not a chance. Every time we activate our mutant genes, the Sentinels know it. I want Magneto to be alive as much as you do, but using our powers to try and find him would be stupid."

"If he's alive, we could use his powers," Ororo said. "He would be a vital part of our plan."

"If we go looking for him and he's dead, we're not going to have any plan at all," Rachel snapped. "You told me to move on. Now the rest of you have to do it, too."

"She's right," Logan said.

"Shouldn't we find out for sure?" Kitty couldn't stand the thought of leaving someone behind. Even if that someone was Magneto! This future…it was too much for her. "How could they do this to me?" she said, without quite meaning to.

"They?" Rachel echoed. "You mean us?

And by us, I mean also your future self. She was full speed ahead on this idea while some of the rest of us were still wavering. So before you go playing the   martyr, consider that. Also consider that Kate is back in the past, hoping to save this whole future from ever happening. Is that worth you being sad, little Kitten?"

"Whoa," Logan said. "Easy. She's just a kid."

"She doesn't get to be just a kid," Rachel said.

"Maybe we should have left you behind, if this is how you're gonna be." Logan pointed at each of the X-Men in turn as he went on. "Who has Storm lost? How about Pete? Kate? Hell, me. You think you're the only one with something to mourn? And you know what else?" Logan swept his arm back to take in the watching FCA soldiers. "These guys have all lost more than any of us, because none of this is their fault. We did it. Mutants. We did it to ourselves. It wasn't norms who killed Kelly and Charlie and Moira. So ditch the sackcloth and ashes, and let's go crack some skulls."

"Speech," said one of the FCA soldiers. A couple of them clapped, whether sincerely or ironically Kitty couldn't tell. But she believed Logan. He stared at Rachel, and she stared right back.

"Have we gotten all of this out of our systems?" Ororo asked, breaking the stalemate. "Rick, you will pardon us for being touchy, I hope. It has been a difficult few hours."

"You bet it has," Rick said. "Maybe we can help you make sure the next few are a bit easier."

The plan, as elaborated by Logan and Rick, was relatively simple. Using the FCA's ability to move about the city, they would assess the Sentinels' security around the Baxter Building. The X-Men would separate into two groups, as Logan had already said. One group would head down the Grand Central-Port Authority shuttle track and come up on 5th Avenue. The other would work its way through maintenance tunnels and surface on Madison near 43rd, using a hole in the street left behind from the Sentinel battle for control of New York. "There were some Rogues in there," Rick said, "but you don't have to worry about them anymore."

In the absence of any telecommunications secure from Sentinel surveillance, the group would work the old-fashioned way, posting individuals at corners along the way and communicating via hand signals. Here they would have help from an unexpected source: The FCA had been cultivating mutant sympathizers from among the ostracized A-class citizens of New York. Many of them were willing to help—although just as many were hostile, seeing the mutants as the reason for their own problems.

"So we set up a network of FCA and these A-class native guides, and that's how we know where we can go and where we can't," Rick said. "We'll get your teams in place."

"And then," Logan finished, "we hit the Baxter Building from two directions, kill every Sentinel we find, and burn that sucker down."

"That ought to tell the Europeans that they should hold off a day or so before they start

dropping bombs, eh?" one of the FCA soldiers
said.

Something about hearing the voices of normal people talking about fighting alongside mutants lightened Kitty's mood. For the first time
since she had arrived in this future, she felt a hint
of hope. No matter how dire the circumstance,
there was still good to be found.

Also, it was the first time she'd ever heard a
Canadian actually say "eh."

CHAPTER 7

THE GUARD was named Reynaldo Cabrera, and he worked the security checkpoint at the garage entrance to one of the Pentagon's many subbasements. Reynaldo did a double take at the size of the guy walking up with Raven Darkholme, one of the secretary of defense's top deputies, whom he saw every day. The two were coming from the underground restricted-access garage just off Jeff Davis Highway. Darkholme's ID badge was clipped to the lapel of her suit, exactly per regulations. The other guy was also wearing a suit—one that looked to the guard's eye like it had been hanging in a closet since about 1978, the year before Cabrera was born. He'd seen pictures of his dad and uncles in suits just like it. Plus the giant was wearing a turtleneck sweater, which put the guard in a bit of a tailspin as he tried to think of the last time he'd seen someone wearing a turtleneck sweater at the Pentagon.

"Good morning, Sergeant Cabrera," Darkholme said.

He snapped off a salute and said, "ID, please, ma'am."

Scanning her ID, he looked expectantly at her…companion? That didn't seem exactly like the right word, because Sergeant Cabrera had just noticed the guy was handcuffed. "And what's our situation with your…?" He let the question hang.

"This is Duke," she said. "It's cleared ahead. Check the Joint Chiefs staff log."

"I'll need his ID, too," Cabrera said.

"I'm afraid they confiscated that at intake," Darkholme said with a smile. Cabrera knew she was flirting with him a little, but he didn't mind. A "Duke Fredericks" was in fact on the pre-approved and cleared Joint Chiefs guest list. Fredericks offered the surliest expression Cabrera had ever seen on a visitor-ID photo.

Cabrera logged Fredericks' arrival and printed a visitor pass. "Keep this on his coat," he said, handing Darkholme the pass. "And I'm afraid that as long as you're in the building with him, both you and he are knocked down a whole bunch of clearance levels."

"Understood, Sergeant. We'll stay on the straight and narrow." She shot him a highly unprofessional wink and led Duke Fredericks into one of the perimeter hallways.

The size of that guy, Cabrera thought. You can practically feel the building shake when he walks.

NEITHER Darkholme nor her companion spoke as they walked nearly the length of the hall and then turned down a side corridor leading to a hospitality suite. The Pentagon maintained them for prolonged meetings and interagency events, as well as the occasional off-the-books visit by dignitaries from allied military services and foreign defense ministries. The occupants of this particular suite, however, were none of those.

As she opened the door, Darkholme's form shimmered and seemed briefly to liquefy before taking the shape of an athletic red-headed woman. In this form, she would have drawn glances wherever she went—especially because of her pupilless eyes and rich blue skin. Her crisp suit was replaced by a form-fitting white dress slit high on both thighs, accented by a waist chain worked in a pattern of skulls. Another skull on her brow brought the whole look together, giving her what she thought was the perfect combination of allure and menace. Her given name was Raven Darkholme, but her enemies in the X-Men knew her as Mystique—though they did not yet know what she was capable of.

She had devoted her adult life to furthering the agenda of the Brotherhood of Mutants, primarily under Magneto's direction. Now, with Magneto buried under a million tons of ice in the Savage Land, Mystique had decided the time had come to reconstitute the Brotherhood—particularly in view of the Hellfire Club's recent resurgence. The Hellfire Club—especially its White Queen, Emma Frost—were now rivals in recruiting mutants and pursuing an agenda opposed to Charles Xavier's. Xavier emphasized a strategy he called coexistence, but Mystique tended to characterize it less charitably as appeasement.

Mystique had visited Max-X the week before in the guise of Blob's lawyer. There she had given him the idea to try the implosion trick that had worked so spectacularly that morning. She had also put out feelers to certain individuals in the Hellfire Club, suggesting that they might do some useful damage to the X-Men if they were present at Max-X on a particular morning.

Then, on the appointed day, Mystique had returned to New Mexico, waiting five miles down the access road at a turnoff that dead-ended into an overgrown logging track. Blob had arrived right on schedule after his dawn breakout, and from there she had gotten him back East with little trouble. Using her Pentagon connections and Brotherhood resources, she created his fake identity. Everything had gone as smoothly as any criminal mastermind could want.

Mystique, however, wasn't a criminal by nature. There were those who might have categorized her as a terrorist, but crime for crime's sake held no interest for her. She wanted mutant power—not to mention power for herself—and she sought to attain that power through a rejuvenated Brotherhood. And what was the best way to increase the strength and power of the Brotherhood? Make a statement of mutant power that no one could ignore. For too long mutants had tried to coexist with those who hated, feared, and persecuted them. This was why she had begun rebuilding the Brotherhood—and why there were three other people already in the suite.

"Good morning, all," she said. "I trust these accommodations meet with your approval. Destiny, Pyro, Avalanche—permit me to introduce Fred Dukes, better known in some circles as the Blob."

"Fred *J.* Dukes," Blob said. Mystique

stopped and locked eyes with him. "Hey," he said after a minute. "That's the name my daddy gave me."

Two of the three other members of the Brotherhood sized up the Blob, then turned to share a smirking glance. Pyro, a rail-thin Englishman with a thick head of hair that made his body look a bit like a just-lighted match, said, "I think I prefer Blob. It's quite a good moniker. Fits you."

"Good thing, too," Avalanche added. He was twice as big as Pyro, blunt and heavy where Pyro was sharp and angular. "Not much else would."

"Gentlemen, this is not a schoolyard. Jokes about size are beneath us." Mystique unlocked Blob's handcuffs, watching him carefully to gauge his reaction to this initial hazing. "And Blob…we try to avoid using our real names, for what should be obvious reasons. With or without middle initial."

For the moment, at least, he appeared unruffled. "Nice digs," he said, crossing to the table and pouring himself a drink. "Also that was one fast ride back from the joint. This is a class operation. Only thing is, I was part of the original Brotherhood, and it seems to me the wrong person's givin' the orders around here."

Ah, Mystique thought. The expected challenge. She let it go, anticipating that Blob's assertion would provoke interesting reactions from the others—and so it did.

"La-de-dah, chunky," Pyro said. "You think you can do better?"

"Blow it out your Union Jack, Limey." Blob paused in the act of lighting a cigar from a crystal box on the bar. Apparently, Mystique had discovered, prohibitions on smoking in federal buildings were relaxed when the presumed occupants had their fingers on their countries' red buttons. "This is between me an'—yeeoww!"

The flame of Blob's match flared and exploded into a monstrous figure, looming over him and singeing his eyebrows. It was gone almost as soon as it appeared, leaving Pyro to comment in his silkiest tone, "Watch your mouth and remember your place—or the next time you light a match, I just might create a demon that will par-boil instead of scare you. This is the new Brotherhood. Magneto is old news."

"Oh yeah?" Blob snatched a marble sculpture from the end of the table. "That's all the lip I'm gonna take from you, pal. Fred J. Dukes ain't no two-bit amateur! You—"

Again Blob broke off—this time because the sculpture had crumbled to dust in his hand.

"Blob," Avalanche said, "have you considered *why* Magneto left you to rot in prison these last few years?"

"Enough, all of you!" Mystique said. "Now you've both shown Blob a little taste of what you can do. Blob, you're correct. I am not Magneto, nor would I wish to be. But cross me—in any way, especially today—and you'll find me as deadly a foe as he ever was to those who betrayed him."

The three men said nothing. Neither did

Destiny. Throughout all this posturing, she had sat quietly in the corner, looking like a librarian or maybe a legal secretary: conservatively cut skirt and coat, nondescript color and style of hair. The only thing that might have made her stand out in a crowd was the dark glasses signaling her blindness. When Mystique issued her threat to Blob, she remained quiet and still—as if nothing more interesting was happening than a conversation about the weather. For Destiny, that was true, since her precognitive abilities had told her what Blob, Pyro, and Avalanche would do before they even knew they were going to do it. Mystique planned to consult with her shortly, but first she had to make a few things clear to the men of the Brotherhood.

"There will be no infighting here. Save it for our enemies." Mystique looked at each of them in turn. "Pyro," she said, "bank your fires. Avalanche, Blob—in case you haven't figured it out, your powers are practically designed so you can't affect each other. Do you think I assembled this particular group by accident?"

"What about her?" Blob said, pointing at Destiny. She hadn't said a word.

"What about her?" Mystique echoed, a mocking lilt in her tone.

"You got an angle on the rest of us. What about her? Who is she, anyway?"

"You'll see. I haven't told anyone everything," Mystique said. "If you believe nothing else, believe that. Now listen to me carefully. We are making a statement today on behalf of all mutants, even those stupid enough to believe that coexistence with nonmutants is possible. We are going to kill Senator Kelly. That part of the operation will be simple. But more importantly, we are going to make something clear to the millions of people who will see this: Mutants will not be oppressed. We will not be bullied. We are taking our fates into our own hands. That means we should not appear to be murderous barbarians."

"Then you should have left him out," Pyro said, nodding at Blob.

"I'm tellin' ya, that's the last—"

"Silence! Both of you! You represent all mutants now. Petty idiocies that interfere with our goals will not be tolerated."

"Very well, then, fearless leader," Pyro said with a mocking smile. "Please. Instruct us."

"I am about to do exactly that," Mystique said. "But first, one more introduction is in order. Blob, this is Destiny."

"Yeah. You told me when we came in."

"What a pleasure to know you were paying attention. Destiny, you know what we are planning to do. Here is where you play your role. Tell us how it will all happen, so we know what to look out for."

But Destiny's face was troubled, and she did not speak.

"What's she do?" Blob asked. "If she catered the room, hey, congratulations. But I'm not hearing anything to make me think we need her."

"What a caveman you are," Pyro said.

"Listen to your betters, and perhaps you will learn something."

For a moment, Blob looked like he might answer Pyro's provocation, but he held himself back. "Seriously," he said. "What's she do?"

"She is a precognitive," Mystique said. Seeing the blank look on Blob's face, she clarified: "Destiny can see the near future before it happens. She can tell us how the police and, potentially, the X-Men in attendance at the hearing will react. She can tell us where everyone in the hearing room will be seated so we know which way to enter, maximizing our chances of success. In a fight like this, that is at least as valuable as the ability to knock down a wall or set a fire."

"We'll see about that," Blob said. "Okay, 'Destiny.' Let's hear it. What's gonna happen?"

Destiny did not answer for a long moment, long enough that all of them grew uncomfortable waiting. Then she said, "I—I am not certain."

CHAPTER 8

THE PLAN, as plans always do, started to go wrong the minute they left the tunnel and headed up from the lower level of Grand Central Terminal to the main concourse, where they planned to split up. Grand Central had long since ceased being a transportation hub, but it was by no means empty. Its former storefronts and kiosks had blended together over the years and gradually become an indoor bazaar, where everything from rice to human beings could be bought and sold. A militia, easy to pick out because of their secondhand fatigues and M-16s, patrolled and kept order.

"Easy to blend in here, soon as we get you some new clothes," Rick said. "Hang on a minute."

He headed into the bazaar and came back fifteen minutes later with an armload of clothing.

"Put it on over your jumpsuits, or change, whatever," he said. "Just don't go running around with a big letter M on your back, right?"

Peter, whose jumpsuit was in shreds, stripped to his skivvies on the spot and put on heavy canvas pants and a thigh-length jacket. "Good guess about the size," he said.

"I bought everything as big as I could get it," Rick said. "Works for you, might not work for some of the others."

Rachel, Storm, and Kitty found this out right away. They wrapped themselves in coats, but none of the other clothes would fit them. "Still, this is better," Storm said. "You're correct that we should avoid identification as mutants, for as long as—"

The Vanderbilt Avenue side of the balcony level exploded inward, burying that end of the concourse under granite and the churned remains of the upstairs level of the bazaar. Spotlights stabbed through the smoke, revealing a Sentinel patrol outside.

"Patrol has encountered escaped mutants," one of them boomed out. "Reinforcements required."

"How did they find us?" Kitty asked. "None of us did anything."

"They've got plain old-fashioned security cameras, too, Kit," Wolverine said. "Here in the station if not in the tunnels. We were never gonna stay hidden forever."

A repulsor beam from one of the Sentinels destroyed a row of booths near an old ticket kiosk. All three Sentinels entered through the hole they'd made in the wall, stepping down from street level to the main concourse.

"Hit 'em, Rach!" Logan called out. "I'll get in close!"

"I can't!" she shouted. "The roof will cave in!"

"You better think of something!" came his reply. Then Logan was gone into the chaos.

"Mutants will be terminated," one of the Sentinels said. Hearing it, a group of militia members pointed, waving their M-16s.

"Those are the escaped muties!" one of them shouted. "Get 'em!"

Ororo had known mutant life was cheap in New York, but she'd assumed other lives had at least a bit more value—until the militia began firing without regard for the bystanders standing between their muzzles and the X-Men and FCA guerrillas. Two of the FCA went down immediately. The rest scattered for cover, returning fire as they could, but handicapped by their unwillingness to take out civilians. The Sentinels, like the militia, charged forward toward their targets.

Ororo picked up Kitty and flew upward, adding fog to the smoke by drawing moisture in from outside and up from the subterranean dampness of the tunnels. Rain began to fall inside the terminal, the sound a constant drumming backdrop to the automatic-weapons fire between the militia and the FCA.

A telepathic message from Rachel made Ororo's eyes water momentarily. *Get into the tunnels, the FCA guy says. They can't follow us there.*

They also can't follow us if they're in pieces, Storm answered. To Kitty she said, "Remember what you did before, at the other station?"

Kitty nodded.

"I'm going to need you to do it again." A repulsor beam burned past them, close enough that rain flashed into steam. Kitty cried out. Still holding on to her, Ororo swooped higher, arcing around behind the Sentinels. "Ready?"

"No!"

"Go anyway!" Ororo said. As she passed over the nearest Sentinel's head, she let Kitty go.

Kitty screamed and the Sentinel looked up at the sound. She landed on its forehead and phased, falling straight down through its head and torso. She emerged from the inside of its left thigh, landing between its feet. Its electrical systems disrupted by Kitty's passage, the Sentinel threw its arms up and started to fall, knocking the Sentinel next to it into a balcony pillar. Kitty dodged out from under the falling robot, straight into a burst from a militia M-16—but Peter, ever watchful over her, interposed his organic-steel body between her and the gunfire. The bullets ricocheted away. Peter charged into the militia, steel fists crushing flesh and bone.

As she always did, Ororo felt a pang of sadness at Peter fight. It was not his nature, and fate was cruel to have made him so good at it.

The second Sentinel braced itself against the edge of the balcony and turned again to look for the mutants. Rachel rocked it with a telekinetic blast that shattered the remaining windows on the balcony level. Then she directed her powers toward the militia, turning their bullets away and flinging the men into the rubble with a push of her mind.

The third Sentinel had forced its way inside and was closing in on them. Logan met it, slashing at its legs and slowing it down. It fell to one knee and smashed an open hand down on Logan. Cracks spread out in the granite floor from the impact. Then the Sentinel lifted its hand; Logan was dangling by one set of his claws from its huge palm. With his other hand, he amputated three of its fingers in a shower of dark fluids before pulling himself free, driving both sets of claws into its midsection and carving it open as he fell.

Storm saw her opening, just as she had on the street before. She drilled a lightning bolt straight into the wound Logan had created, blowing the Sentinel back out through the hole onto Vanderbilt Avenue. But that took her attention away from the remaining active Sentinel, which swatted her out of the air to smash into the balcony façade directly over Kitty's head.

Storm hit the ground limp and bloodied. Kitty ran to her, along with four FCA guerrillas. "We have to get out of here!" Rick shouted. "Now! Into the tunnels!" He shouldered his rifle and picked up Storm, running for the stairs that led back to the lower level. His soldiers followed, and so did Kitty, with Logan close behind. Peter and Rachel came last, Peter shielding them as best he could from the militia's last volleys.

At the top of the stairs, Rachel turned. "I'm not done yet," she said. Gunfire chipped the wall over her head.

"Not a good time, Rachel!" Logan shouted up the stairs.

She ignored him, focusing a second telekinetic pulse on the last remaining Sentinel. The impact caved in its torso and blew one of its arms off. Behind it, another section of the balcony collapsed. The Sentinel, falling, took the brunt of the cascading granite on its head and shoulders.

Rachel watched her handiwork a moment too long, and a burst of gunfire chopped through the upper part of the stairwell. Blood spattered the wall at the head of the stairs; Rachel stumbled forward and fell, tumbling down the steps. Peter charged to meet her, but she slipped out of his grasp and slid another few stairs down. He turned, slipping on blood, and bent to pick her up.

A group of militia appeared at the head of the stairs. Peter gathered Rachel up, hunching over her and pressing himself against one wall as he dropped down the last few stairs. From around the corner at the base of the stairwell, along the opposite wall, some of the FCA guerrillas fired at the militia, putting one man down and scattering the rest.

Firing blindly from his stomach, one of the militiamen hit Peter square in the back of the head. He shook it off. "I've got her! Let's go!"

They ran. Rick led the way, with the X-Men following close behind and the rest of the surviving FCA guerrillas taking turns carrying Ororo. The FCA kept an eye out for militia pursuit, but there wasn't any, and the Sentinels couldn't get to the deeper tunnels. Once the group reached the lowest level of old tracks coming out of Grand Central, they paused.

Rick walked back to Peter with a flashlight and trained it on the limp Rachel. "Let's get a look at her."

"What about Ororo?" Kate asked.

"I'll be all right," Ororo said. "Just a little bruised."

"Damn, lady," one of the guerrillas said. "Way you hit that wall, I figured we were bringing you along just to bury you."

Ororo smiled. "Not today. At least not yet. You—are all your soldiers here, Rick?"

He shook his head. "Lost four. Anyone else need attention?"

"Look after the redhead first," one of the guerrillas said, indicating Rachel. The left arm of his coat was shining and dark with blood.

"JP, take a look at Marc," Rick said. "We've got enough Band-Aids to go around." He helped Peter set Rachel down gently. She opened her eyes, but not all the way. Rick probed gently under her coverall, pausing a couple of times as she gasped in pain. He stood up and took a step back, to where Logan was waiting.

"If you have something to say to her, better say it now," Rick said quietly.

Ororo heard and came to join them, moving slowly and stiffly. "Are you certain?" she asked.

"She might not make it even if we could get

her to a hospital," Rick said. "As it is—"

"I can hear you talking about me," Rachel said.

"No telepathy," Logan said. "Sentinels, remember?"

"You're right," Rachel said. "Okay. But I won't be around for them to track in an hour." She caught her breath and tensed, closing her eyes. "Or…maybe not that long."

Blood pooled under her. Peter's arms and legs were slick with it from carrying her.

"Are you…well, I guess you're sure, aren't you?" Ororo asked.

Rachel nodded. Her eyes were starting to close. "Hey, Rach," Logan said. "Stay with us. Rick'll get you patched up."

Rick looked up at him, then back to what he was doing. The bandages he applied turned red as fast as he could put them on her.

"Don't think so, Logan," Rachel said. "I'll… I'll try to hang on long enough to send Kitty back. But make it fast, okay?"

"Rick," Logan said, "whatever the timetable

was before, change everything to right now."

"Got it. We're ready to go."

Peter still looked troubled. "I remember when the Sentinels seemed to be just robots. These…they have minds. That makes killing them a little different."

"Not to me," Logan said. "I've killed plenty of things with minds. And we're about to kill more, unless you want all of our minds to be fallout blowing over the North Atlantic. Come on. If Magneto's still around, he'll find us."

"He's in a wheelchair, Logan. How's he going to get anywhere to find us?" Rachel asked.

Logan grinned. "You didn't know him as well as we did. All of you ditched your collars, right? Right. Well, Magneto got out of Auschwitz alive. He got out of the Savage Land alive. He got out of freakin' Battleworld alive. Now, if he made it out of the South Bronx alive, you think transportation's gonna be a problem for him? Let's go." Logan tapped Rick on the shoulder. "Can we move her? We can't stay here."

"Buddy, it's not gonna make any difference what you do to her at this point," Rick said. "Sorry."

"You can move me," Rachel said. "I'll… hold myself together, at least for a while."

"I'm afraid you can't," Ororo said. "If you use your powers, the Sentinels will know where we are."

"Then I'm going to die pretty soon, Ororo," Rachel said.

Ororo nodded. "I know. That's why we have to keep moving."

Rick finished placing pressure bandages over Rachel's wounds. Peter picked her up, holding her against his chest while Rick bound her to him with strips of cloth. "The less she bounces around, the less she'll bleed," he said. "So…"

"I understand," Peter said.

"Okay, gang," Logan said. "New plan. We were gonna wait until we had the whole thing set up with all our A-class sympathizers up-stairs. But whatever we do now, we need to do it while Rachel can still send Kitty back." He looked at the FCA guerrillas. "I'll explain that part later, if there is a later."

He ticked off names on his fingers. "Still two teams: me and 'Roro on one, Pete and Rachel and Kate on the other. I'll go first with 'Ro, give you guys a chance to get Rachel settled somewhere. Then you come running. Rick's boys are gonna—"

"And girls," one of the FCA guerrillas interrupted.

"And girls," Logan amended, "are gonna crash the building right behind me and 'Ro. You don't want to tangle with the Sentinels, but any human walking in that building is fair game. We do whatever we can to shut down the Baxter Building. If we don't, we're all gonna be dead this time tomorrow, no matter what the Sentinels do."

"Hell of a pep talk," Rick said.

"Pep's not one of my virtues, bub," Logan said. "The Sentinels've got every advantage in the world—except we're fighting to survive, and who knows what the hell good that will do us. We ready to go, or should I try to make everybody feel better first?"

"Ready as we're gonna get," Rick said.

Logan started walking. "Then let's do it."

CHAPTER 9

WHAT do you mean, you aren't certain?" Mystique snapped. "How could you be certain when I left for New Mexico last night and uncertain at noon today?"

Pyro, Avalanche, and Blob were watching, and she could already feel each of them figuring angles. If her plan wasn't going the way it was supposed to, she could expect challenges sooner rather than later. Pyro especially concerned her. Avalanche and Blob were bruisers, but he was a schemer.

"Something has changed," Destiny said simply.

"What?"

"There is…uncertainty."

Mystique froze. A long moment passed. "What kind of uncertainty?"

"A variable has been introduced. I do not know its nature."

"How long ago was this variable introduced?"

"This morning. Before that, all was clear. All was as we wished it to be. Now…" Destiny looked troubled. She did not like uncertainty, was offended by variables and probabilities. Mystique could tell she was frankly terrified by the idea that her precognitive powers might be vulnerable to sudden changes in external factors. "Now there is…I cannot be certain what will happen."

"Focus," Mystique said. "We have been friends long enough that I know when you are not entirely present. We need you if we are to accomplish the Brotherhood's mission here."

"The problem is not a lack of focus on my part. It is, rather, the refusal of one variable to settle itself."

"What the hell is she goin' on about?" Blob demanded.

"All people have infinite futures," Destiny

said, "if one looks far enough ahead. But in the near term, over hours or days, their actions are circumscribed by thousands of other events taking place around them and removing the vast majority of their potential actions. I see what remains following this winnowing of possibilities. But now, as of this morning, something new has appeared in the future. A…doubling, perhaps? That is not exactly the right word. The important thing is that where I saw certainty, now there is doubt. Someone today will act in an unexpected manner, and there is no way for me to reduce the possibilities beyond a final either-or. And before you say it, Blob, let me just advise you to remain silent."

Blob sneered. "You just got through tellin' us you don't know what's gonna happen, but you know what I was gonna say?"

Destiny smiled. "Exactly. You are gathering your courage right now to say something you think will advance your position within the group by demeaning what you see as my failure.

But doing that will exceed Raven's patience and will elicit consequences for you. Believe me, they are not consequences you wish to suffer. So you will not say it."

Blob opened his mouth, then shut it again. Pyro snickered.

"You don't know nothin' about Fred J. Dukes," Blob said.

"Believe that if you wish," Destiny said, still wearing her condescending smile.

"Who is this variable? One of us?" Mystique asked.

"I do not believe so," Destiny said. "We are all as we were: creatures of this moment in time, and only this moment. But there is another, who has…changed. That change has disrupted the possibilities."

This morning, Mystique thought. It hardly seemed possible that Destiny's sudden uncertainty and the X-Men's jaunt out to Max-X after Blob's breakout could be a coincidence.

Had something happened during the Hellfire

Club's ambush of the X-Men? Mystique ran through the possibilities. Had word gotten to Xavier somehow? That wasn't possible. No one knew of the Brotherhood's plan except the five people in this room. Had some of the X-Men been killed? That would make no difference to the hearings. Senator Kelly would merely use it as an occasion to paint them posthumously as dangerously out-of-control vigilantes.

Was *Blob* the uncertainty? She couldn't believe that. He was exactly what he appeared to be: a hypermassive slab of humanity, his speech and demeanor as coarse as his limbs were powerful. A blunt instrument. Nothing about him was uncertain. You didn't have to have Destiny's precognitive abilities to be sure what the Blob would do in any given situation.

Who, then?

She did not know who the X-Men had sent to New Mexico, but which of the X-Men could destabilize probabilities enough to interfere with Destiny? The Scarlet Witch was the only mutant with that ability, and she was not a member of the X-Men. Still...

Mystique placed a quick call to a source on the staff at Max-X and learned that the Scarlet Witch had not been seen in New Mexico. Her source did complain that the X-Men had completely overwhelmed the Hellfire Club—but not only was that not Mystique's problem, she was glad to hear it. The more the Hellfire Club and X-Men focused on each other, the more room the Brotherhood had to carry out her plans.

The death of Senator Kelly was just the beginning. Magneto had once envisioned the Brotherhood ruling the world, empowering mutants to take their rightful place in control of normal humans—those unfortunates whose genomes had done nothing more interesting than predispose them to heart disease or give them red hair. Mystique intended to succeed where Magneto had failed.

First the Brotherhood would announce itself and fire a symbolic shot across the bow of humanity by silencing the most strident anti-mutant voice in the United States government. Some mutants would rally to the Brotherhood. Others would cower behind Xavier. Mystique would face the X-Men—and destroy them. Then, a united mutantkind would end thousands of years of this ridiculous upside-down way of things, with normal humans reigning over mutants…oppressing them…massacring them…

United mutantkind would rule the world. As befitted their superiority. And at the head of mutantkind would stand Mystique, ruling over all.

That was the task they were beginning today, whether or not Destiny's vision was cloudy.

"This changes nothing," Mystique said. "Robert Kelly dies today. So, too, does anyone who opposes us. Perhaps, to remove even more uncertainty, we should eliminate Xavier and MacTaggert, as well."

"I have anticipated this speculation," Destiny said. "The existing irreducible variable is not affected."

"As distasteful as I find it to agree with Fred J. Dukes," Pyro said, "now I too find myself wanting to know exactly what she's on about."

"Yeah," Avalanche said. "Do we know what's going to happen or not?"

"We will attack the Senate," Destiny said. "That much is still certain."

"That's all we need," Mystique said.

"With all due respect, Raven, the situation is quite different if our pet precognitive here can no longer fulfill her role," Pyro said. "It is one thing to attack the Senate and perform an assassination when we have anticipated the outcome. It is quite another to mount such an attack when we find ourselves stripped of the predictive powers that gave us our advantage."

"Nah, that don't matter," Blob said. "We go in, we bust stuff up, we do the job on Kelly. The rest of it don't matter."

"He curries favor after his bluster is unrewarded," Pyro said. "How predictable. Am I right, Destiny? Oh, pardon me. You don't know anymore, do you?"

"Here is what *I* know," Mystique said. "At the appointed time, we are going to walk out this door and make our way to the rear of the Hart Building. Then everyone will do what they are supposed to do. Whoever does not, will answer to me…after Senator Kelly is dead, and the world once again learns to fear the Brotherhood."

Her form shifted again; a moment later Raven Darkholme, top Defense Department advisor, stood before them once more. "Would anyone like to share their misgivings?" she asked. Her tone made it clear that she expected only silence in return. "Good," she said. "Then let's go."

AS THEY passed by his station on their way out, Sergeant Cabrera said, "Have a good day, Ms. Darkholme."

"You too, Sergeant." She smiled and returned the visitor pass for Duke Frederickson. She had three more people with her now, and Cabrera said, "Hold on there a minute. I need all of your visitor passes back, please."

Something had melted part of one of the passes. Cabrera looked up at the wiry blond Englishman who had given it to him. "What were you guys doing in there? Interrogations happen in another part of the building," he joked.

"Oh, we had a bit of a heated discussion," the Englishman said. According to the pass, his name was St. John Allerdyce. Cabrera had read somewhere that the name was pronounced Sinjin, but something about the man's demeanor stopped him from asking. One of the other passes, for Jon Bloom, was covered in some kind of fine dust. He saw Ms. Darkholme watching as he passed a chemical-sensing pad over it.

"Is there a problem, Sergeant?" she asked, her tone managing to be both friendly and threatening.

That set him on edge a little, that know-your-place tone he heard all too often from civilians. After they'd gone to Afghanistan and dodged RPGs for two years, they could talk to him like that. Not before. "Procedures, ma'am," he said, and put the chemically sensitive pad through a scanner at the checkpoint workstation.

The scan came up negative, so that was that. Darkholme probably wouldn't shoot him a wink next time she came in, but Cabrera didn't care. He had a job to do. "Enjoy your day, folks," he said and watched the five of them head out the door.

Irene Adler, the other woman with Ms. Darkholme, looked to be blind, but she walked like she could see. Weird bunch, Cabrera thought. Not like the policy wonks and officers Darkholme usually traveled with.

He wondered what kind of project she was involved in. Her record showed work with DARPA and other weapons stuff, which explained the motley group of civilians. Defense was a pretty buttoned-down outfit, but their contractors—especially the ones working on far-out tech—tended to be T-shirt-and-sandal types with their heads in the clouds. Except Tony Stark, Cabrera thought. Now that was a guy with style. He'd gotten Stark's autograph once, when the man himself stopped by the Pentagon for a meeting. It was at home in one of Cabrera's scrapbooks. When his kids were old enough to read, he'd show it to them and say: *I met that guy. That's what you should want to be when you grow up.*

That wasn't something he'd ever say about Jon Bloom or Irene Adler or St. John Allerdyce. Or especially Duke Frederickson. Takes all kinds, Cabrera thought. But you have to be careful who you choose as your role models.

Cabrera had standing orders to report to his superiors whenever a staff member did something unusual, and he was starting to think that this was one of those times. Plenty of contractors came and went in the Pentagon, and Duke Frederickson wasn't the first person he'd seen come in wearing handcuffs. But the whole scene struck him as…off.

He wrote down the names of all the visitors and ran them through the system, looking to see whether any of them had ever been in the building before. He also ran facial-recognition scans on the photos he'd taken for their visitor passes.

No alerts came up.

Still, Cabrera had an uneasy feeling. The melted pass, and the powder…he decided to do the safe thing, which was kick it up the chain of command. All four passes and a printout of the entry and exit times went into a sealed envelope, with a report documenting Cabrera's feeling that something out of the ordinary might be going on. His superiors could ignore it, and God knew they probably would, but he was doing this one by the book.

He finished the report, sealed it in the envelope with the passes, and put it in the box for the interoffice mail to pick up. When shift change came around and he headed for the cafeteria to grab a sandwich, he was relieved—both emotionally and professionally. Something about working in the Pentagon made a guy suspicious.

CHAPTER 10

GRAND Central Terminal was only a couple of blocks from the Baxter Building, so the final stage of the team's mission prep didn't involve much travel. They followed the disused track to a juncture where maintenance hatches went up a level, somewhere around the intersection of Vanderbilt and 45th. From there, they planned to proceed west one short block to Madison, then double back south. At 42nd, they would split up. Logan and Storm would continue on to the Fifth Avenue subway station with some of the FCA guerrillas while Rachel, Peter, and Kate waited.

"Once the fireworks start," Logan said, "Petey can come on in and join the fun."

"What about me?" Kitty said.

"You're staying with Rachel so she can send you home once everything is on track," Ororo said.

"Wait a minute. That wasn't what we decided before, was it?"

"Kitten, you've got a life to live. Part of why we're doing this is so you can live it. We brought you here without meaning to because we needed to send Kate back...but you don't need to suffer for that." Ororo looked at Peter, prompting him.

"Ororo is right, Kitty," he said. "This is not your time. Whatever happens here, we fight so you will have a different future."

She knew there was something he wasn't telling her, though, and she wasn't prepared to let it go. "Why did you want him to say that, Ororo? Why does everyone look at us funny? Will someone explain to me what's going on?"

"Petey, this one's all yours," Logan said.

"Kitty, in this future...you and I have been married for some time. It is difficult for me, telling you this. When I look at you, I see my wife. But I know that you are just a girl on the inside, and..." Peter ran out of words. "It is difficult. I do not wish it to be difficult for you, as well."

"We're *married?*" Kitty repeated. She couldn't fathom it. Married? And when he saw her, he…?

She looked down at herself, her adult body, with its twenty-two extra years of life that she had never experienced. Every feeling in the world seemed to rush through her at once. Anger that no one had told her before. Confusion about futures overlaid, lived and unlived. Uncertainty about how she would feel toward Peter when she got home, and he was so much younger, and she knew this, and he didn't. How could she talk to him? How would she…? And then, deep revulsion that Peter must have been…

"No," she said. "That's…why did you tell me that?"

"You asked," Logan said.

"Then, then, you should get Kate back," Kitty said. "Rachel should…" She stumbled, realizing she was just about to argue the exact opposite of what she'd been arguing a moment before. "How am I supposed to deal with this?"

"Good question," Logan said.

"Very good question," Peter said. "I do not have an answer. It is my hope that we will do this, and survive, and you will go home. Then whatever happens in that past…in your future…will either happen or not. We may change something, we may change everything, we may change nothing."

"Whoa," Rick said. "Deep."

"Easy for you to say," Kitty said. "You don't have to go back."

"But you do. Which is why we do not want you in the fight. If you were to be killed, God forbid, not only would you die, but we do not know what would happen to Kate." For the only time she could remember—but of course, she hadn't known him that long—Kitty saw fear on Peter's face. He was on the verge of tears.

"Hey," she said. "If my other self…my future me, or this me in the future…if she chose you, she made a pretty good choice." She paused. "Not that I'm doing that. Um."

"Let's talk about something else, shall we?" Ororo suggested.

"Like maybe how we all plan to live through the next hour," Logan said.

"Most of us, anyway," Rachel said. She had gotten paler even in the last twenty minutes, since Peter had started carrying her.

With a sick pang of fear, Kitty realized that Rachel might be too weak to send her back when the time came. But she said nothing. The stakes, she realized, were life and death—and not just for them. Whatever happened to the five X-Men, that fate would be writ large in the destiny of all humankind.

It was time to bear down and do what needed to be done. But there was one more thing Kitty couldn't get out of her mind. "If Rachel can't fight, and you don't want me to fight," she said, "don't we need Magneto?"

"Love to *have* him," Logan said. "Going to get him, not so much."

"But that's not right," Kitty said. "He helped you get free. We can't just go off and leave him."

Logan walked over and got right in her face.

"What do you mean, can't? We can't do anything else. Unless you want to surrender, maybe, and you can get used to camp life the way your grown-up self did. How's that sound, Kit-Kat?"

"Logan, you need to remember you're talking to a thirteen-year-old girl," Ororo said.

"You want to know what I was doing when I was thirteen? You can be damn sure nobody sugarcoated anything for me," Logan said. "And anyway, we don't know if he's alive. Assuming he didn't get nuked after he fell out of his chair, and assuming he remembered how to use all his powers, and assuming he wasn't too old to fight…he might be. If he is, he knows the plan. He either gets here or he doesn't."

"Okay, you want to be tough? I can be tough, too," Kitty said. "If you don't want to go get Magneto, I'll go myself."

"Don't write any checks you can't cash, kid," Logan said. "You don't even know the way."

"I can read a map," Kitty said. "I can get to the Bronx. And from there I can find him."

"Before or after the Rogues find you?"

"I don't care. I'm going."

Logan grabbed her arm, but Kitty phased out of his grip.

"Don't, Kitten! The Sentinels!" Ororo said.

"Crap—she used her power. Now we have to move." Logan spat on the tunnel floor. "Teenagers. Listen, kid. I'll make this quick so we can get moving before your little tantrum gets us all killed. Rachel's not gonna live long enough for you to get home if we go after him. That's just the plain truth."

"I don't care," Kitty said again, although she did care. She cared about that more than just about anything else. If Rachel died, Kitty Pryde was never going to feel her own body grow up. She was never going to see any of her friends again. She would, in all probability, die sometime within the next twenty-four hours, either from a Sentinel weapon or a nuclear explosion. She cared.

And she cared enough about these battered,

cynical, doomed versions of her friends that she was racked with guilt about having used her powers. They all stared at her, waiting for her— for the kid, the teenager, the flighty one, the one who threw tantrums—to get her act together.

So she did. "I'm sorry," she said. "I didn't mean to…you know."

"Problem isn't whether you meant to. Problem is you did it," Logan said.

"I know, I know," Kitty said, miserable, and then Rachel cut in and said, "Give the kid a break, Logan. I'm doing it, too…using my power to hold myself together."

"Rachel, stop it right now. I mean it," Storm said.

"Can't," Rachel said, shaking her head. "If I do, you'll be carrying a body by the time we get to the end of this tunnel."

"Maybe we will and maybe we won't, but if you keep that up we'll all be bodies for someone to carry."

"Don't think so," Rachel said. "Just my body

talking to itself. I'm real quiet when I have to be."

"See?" Kitty said. "I can be quiet, too. Look at us! We lost Franklin. We won't have Rachel much longer. You don't think we could use Magneto in this fight? Or are you just too damn stubborn to listen to me because I'm a kid?"

"Watch your mouth there, Kitten, or Pete's gonna wash it out with soap."

"I hate to say this," Ororo said, "but Logan's right."

"Ororo," Kitty said. "I thought—"

"Listen to me. You're right that we need Magnus. You're right that we are depleted. You're right that going after him is the ethical thing to do, and that it will weigh on our collective conscience for the rest of our lives if we do not go back and try to save him. But hear these words again: *the rest of our lives.*

"How long is that going to be if we do not destroy the Baxter Building? And do we have the strength to face the entire Sentinel garrison in the Bronx? Can we survive that and still get back here in time to avert the missile strikes from Europe? No, Kitten, we can't. So the only way we can save Magneto is if we go in and take out the Sentinel nerve center in the Baxter Building. Once that is done, everything else becomes possible; until it is done, we can do nothing else."

"And we need to do it now, before the Sentinels peel the roof off this tunnel," Logan said. The FCA soldiers looked up nervously.

"It's not right," Kitty said.

"The minute we can, we'll go get him. If he's still alive."

Kitty nodded. She could see Ororo's point, and Logan's, even though she hated to admit it. And she'd done a dumb thing, phasing like that. She wasn't holding it together—and if she didn't shape up, a lot of people were going to get killed. Knowing that Rachel was also violating the no-powers rule made her feel a little better—but only a little.

She wondered what Magneto was doing right then, if he was even still alive. She had to admit it was pretty unlikely. All those Sentinels, against one old man…

"Let's go, then," she said.

"'Bout time," Logan said and started to lead them to the west.

IT WAS a misperception, Magnus thought, that the powers of mutants were limitless. That idea, that mutants were inexhaustible machines rather than people who grew tired, careless, sad—it contributed to the unease and fear many nonmutants felt toward his kind. He knew this because he had heard it firsthand from haters of mutants, from demagogues and well-meaning rabble-rousers, all of them convinced that a quirk in a mutant's genome meant somehow that none of the rules of the natural world applied anymore. The questions they had asked him…Do you sleep? Do you require food? Are you indestructible? And so forth.

No one cared about what it was like to be literally one in a million, marked out from the

rest of your species by a particular, unique ability. Everyone gawked at difference, but no one
wanted to be different. Not really. They wanted
to dress differently, paint themselves differently,
ink different designs in their skin—but *real* difference was beyond them, and so those who tru-
ly were different seemed…well, like gods. And
that, Magnus admitted, was a delusion too many
mutants had agreed to share.

But it was not the case. Even when he had
been at his peak, he remembered the feeling of
slippage—when his mind and body grew weary of
battle, and eventually even the will began to surrender. He was not at that point now, but he was
also not as strong as he once had been. He was an
old man, with his hundredth birthday gone by—
spent with a single candle on a rare loaf of fresh
bread, with Peter improvising Russian lyrics to
"Happy Birthday" and everyone clapping in an ev-
anescent moment of joy. It would stand out to him
forever, that moment.

But it was gone. And he was tired. He was

an old man, his powers diminished, and he was too tired even to lift himself from the ground. One more task yet remained before him, and he did not know whether he would recover quickly enough to perform it.

Magneto had earned his fatigue. The Sentinel garrison of the South Bronx Mutant Internment Center was reduced to scrap. Some of them had been blown to pieces when he forced their individual components to repel each other. Others had imploded when he increased the attraction of those same sets of components. He had dismembered one Sentinel as it lifted off, squawking warnings and threatening to bring in reinforcements.

Magneto had waited twenty years to unleash his fury on the Sentinels. This was a good beginning, but he was not done yet.

The fences of the camp were gone. He had coiled them around the Sentinels, who now lay incapacitated in the streets surrounding the camp. He was the last mutant in the Mutant

Internment Center, but not the last person. More than ninety percent of the inmates here were nonmutant criminals and undesirables, held officially in a parallel institution blandly designated the South Bronx Processing Center. These criminals were in full-scale riot— sacking and destroying camp facilities, and killing the staff.

Magneto did nothing to stop them. He had no sympathy for those who had chosen to work with the Sentinels. Any of the prisoners at Auschwitz would have done the same to him during his days as a *Sonderkommando*, and they would have been fully justified.

Other humans had escaped instead of waiting around to exact revenge. Fires burned, people screamed. Groups ran back and forth across the open grounds, carrying equipment and God only knew what else from the camp facilities.

A band of rioters saw him, dragging himself across the ground. "Hey, look, the wheelchair mutie doesn't have his chair," one of them said.

From his right hand dangled a length of two-by-four, bent nails still sticking out of the end where he had twisted it free of whatever structure it had once been part of.

With a flick of his wrist, Magneto drove the nails into the man's forehead. He let out a long whistling sigh, bit down on his tongue, and sagged to the ground.

Magneto turned to the others. "I have freed you," he said. "But if you would prefer, I can kill you here. It makes no difference whatsoever to me. Decide now."

They ran back into the fury of the riot.

To the northwest, Magneto saw the flares of Sentinel booster rockets. Reinforcements. They would arrive before he was finished, but that problem could wait. There was one task yet to complete before he could leave this camp for the last time.

He dragged himself closer to the smoldering ruin of the camp command center. As he drew nearer to it, he used its metal frame to attract him, speeding his progress. He moved through the command center, not expending the energy it would have taken to magnetically levitate—he would need every erg and joule later—but instead pulling himself along the smooth tile floor into the medical facility.

There he found a stainless-steel surgical table. With a wave he peeled away a portion of it and shaped it to fit his head. It hung in the air as he turned it back and forth and decided it would do. The color was wrong, but this was not the time to quibble over aesthetics. He reached his left hand toward the bank of computers and diagnostic instruments lining one wall of the examination room. They began to disassemble themselves, screws popping loose and welds breaking. He drew wires together, arranged them on the inside surface of the helmet, sealed them in place. Then a second layer of sheet metal from the examination table formed the inside of the helmet.

He brought it to himself, felt its cold weight

in his hands. When he put it on, a smile broke across his face.

Yes, he thought. The final destiny of this future is still to be determined.

There was enough left of the table surface to separate into strips. He formed those strips to fit into the soles of his boots, with smaller pieces worked into the linings of his camp coverall. When he was done, he felt exhausted. He had not used his powers in almost twenty years, and his concentration was lagging. But there was another, much greater task yet to be performed. He could not rest yet.

He closed his eyes, feeling the flow and surge of that most intimate of universal forces: electromagnetism. Yes, he thought. At last.

And Magneto rose from the floor. He gestured at the ceiling, and the steel beams holding it up lifted away, tearing loose the roof and exposing a sky thick with smoke. He rose above the destroyed building and saw two Sentinels, the first of the reinforcements, settling into their work of annihilating the rioters. He seized both of them and lifted them into the air, repelling them from the Earth itself.

He held them for a moment as they recognized him. "Mutant 067—" one of them began, but he did not let it finish.

"Magneto," he corrected the Sentinel. He said it again, louder—*"Magneto!"*—and brought the two Sentinels crashing together with an inward sweep of his arms. He repeated his name and hammered the Sentinels together until the ground below them was littered with broken-off pieces of their armor. Both Sentinels hung limp, dangling lazily in the air from invisible strings of magnetic force.

"Never again," Magneto said, and let them fall.

He floated out over the devastated grounds of the camp. He saw what he had done and found it good. The work, however, was not yet complete. As long as he stayed here, more Sentinels would come.

The Baxter Building, he thought. Perhaps I

cannot walk. Perhaps I will never walk.

But now, once again, I can fly.

CHAPTER 11

RIGHT on schedule, the Blackbird touched down at a private airport in the D.C. suburbs. Warren Worthington, Angel, was there to meet them with a helicopter, and ten minutes later they were disembarking from it at a private helipad attached to one of his many penthouse condominiums. All of them were in civilian clothing, not wishing to draw attention to themselves—although Angel, with his movie-star looks and immense wealth, could not avoid attention wherever he went. And that was before one took into account the magnificent sixteen-foot span of the wings that gave him his code name.

According to Angel, Charles Xavier was already in the Senate hearing room waiting for the proceedings to begin. Angel had been monitoring Hellfire Club activity and helping Xavier and

Moira MacTaggert prep for the Senate hearings.

"Emma Frost and the Hellfire Club are still after Kitty, in case you were wondering," he said. "You know Emma, the minute someone tells her no…"

"The Hellfire Club is an irritation, Warren," Ororo said. "We have more pressing problems at the moment. Get us to the hearing. I'll fill you in along the way."

At first, like the rest of them, Angel didn't believe the story. "She's traumatized," he said, gesturing at Kate. "Xavier's going to tell you the same thing when we get there. Then he'll point out that there are problems we need to handle ourselves—without always going to him for advice. So how about we just handle this ourselves?"

"Sure. Let's do that," Kate said. "Then when the Sentinels kill you in 2021, I'll get to smell your wings burning all over again."

"Is she going through a Goth phase?" Angel asked Ororo.

"I'm right here, Warren. You can talk to me

like I'm a scared kid if you want to—but three hours ago by my internal clock I was smuggling the last piece of the Jammer into the camp, and Logan had just saved my life from the Rogues. I walked by your tombstone on my way to our quarters. Make fun of me all you want."

He looked at her, then at Logan, then back to Ororo. "Well, she's serious. I guess the least we can do is try to make it to the hearing before everything gets started, so Xavier can rummage around in her head."

They got into a limo waiting in front of the condominium tower. Angel told the driver their destination, then rolled up the window divider.

"After we see the Professor, you can apologize," Kate said.

"For what?" Warren asked.

"For not believing me."

"I don't know about that, little Kitty. Even if your story turns out to be true, which it won't, you can hardly expect me to apologize for being rational."

"Rationally address this, then," Ororo said. "There was a Sentinel at Max-X. Someone is playing on Senator Kelly's misgivings to convince authorities to deploy Sentinels again. That would be ominous even if we did not have Kitty's story to deal with."

"Agreed," Warren said. "We'll address that. But I don't have to believe fairy tales about mind-swaps and time travel to know the Hellfire Club and Sentinels are a threat. We've got enough problems without buying into every crazy story that comes along."

Logan hadn't said a word since landing the Blackbird, but now he did. "You'll see, bub."

"Will I? She's convinced even you?"

"Not all the way. But enough to think we'd better get to this hearing sooner rather than later."

Warren looked to Kurt. "What about you, *mein Freund?* You don't believe this, do you?"

"I do," Kurt said. "I think you would, too, if you had seen the change in her when it happened."

Warren had access to restricted parking

areas, either because of his own influence or because Xavier was on the day's witness list. The group spilled out of the limousine and entered through a security checkpoint far from the public areas of the building— except for Logan and Kurt, who preferred to stay out of the public eye. The group paused in the lobby to watch the introductory proceedings on a closed-circuit monitor.

The chamber was packed, as it always was for hearings on issues that lent themselves to rabble-rousing. Hearings on policy were conducted before jaded audiences of reporters and policy wonks. But change the topic to social issues, and loud voices came out of the woodwork to clog up the gallery and interrupt the proceedings with staged sloganeering.

For this occasion, anti-mutant protesters had crowded into the gallery, bearing placards and chanting at a volume just below a level that would get them kicked out under the Senate's rules. Those rules were somewhat arbitrary, but the anti-mutant group seemed to have rehearsed their behavior—or else the Senate bailiffs had some sympathy for the anti-mutant point of view.

The floor of the hearing chamber was a rectangular space walled in on three sides by galleries. On the fourth side, a long table on a raised dais ran along the wall, facing another long table placed in front of the first row of gallery seats. Behind the raised table were ten senators—the members of the Senate Special Committee on Superhuman Security—and a single empty chair belonging to Senator Robert Kelly. Kelly was pacing around the chamber, grandstanding for all he was worth.

At the witness table, Charles Xavier and Moira MacTaggert waited for him to finish his introductory remarks. Xavier was his usual collected self, impeccably dressed, not a drop of sweat on his shaven head even under the blazing lights of a dozen television crews. Ororo recognized his favorite green blanket draped over his legs. Moira, equally at ease, sat next to Xavier wearing the tailored suit of an aristocrat and the practical haircut of a researcher who needed to keep her hair out of the samples. Both remained impassive, but Ororo was fairly certain that if she had Xavier's telepathic gifts, she would be hearing a number of unflattering things about the Senator.

"We are gathered here to address an issue of critical national and international importance," Kelly was saying. "This is not a witch hunt, but— we hope and pray—a search for truth. Much about our world has changed. We face situations—and threats—undreamed-of by earlier generations."

Kelly paced as he spoke, angling to deliver parts of his speech to each of the three gallery areas while keeping his face visible to at least one TV camera at all times. "One such change is the appearance of so-called Homo superior." He lingered over those last two words, making his disapproval clear and taking a breath before going on. "Mutants! Flesh of our flesh, blood of our blood, yet possessing powers and abilities which set them apart from—some, including many mutants themselves, would say *above*—the rest of humanity.

"Among our witnesses today is Professor Charles Xavier—world-renowned expert on genetics and unabashed advocate for mutants, including his protégés known as the X-Men. We also have Doctor Moira MacTaggert of Edinburgh University, whose work on human genetics and the mechanics of genetic mutation has won—deservedly, in my mind—the Nobel Prize. Doctors Xavier and MacTaggert, thank you very much for coming."

"Pleasure," Charles said.

"Happy to be here," Moira said, although her expression suggested precisely the opposite.

There was a rustle in the gallery as several of the X-Men entered. Ororo, Peter, Kitty, and Warren made their way to a block of seats reserved as a courtesy for friends and supporters of those called to testify. Some of the anti-mutant protesters recognized them and muttered a stream of vitriol, just below the volume that would have brought the bailiffs over.

Warren led the group. Ororo believed that his fame and photogenic profile would draw attention from the rest of them, placing the entire team in the best possible light. Cynical, perhaps, but she was learning that managing the X-Men's image in the public eye was in some ways more important to their survival than opposing the Brotherhood.

Or at least that had been true until today, if Kate Pryde was to be believed. On that score, Ororo was still uncertain. She inclined toward believing Kate, but she also had long ago learned to trust Logan's instincts. She was conflicted.

Logan himself was not at the hearing. Nor was Nightcrawler. Neither of them, particularly Kurt, provided what the PR professionals called good optics. Kurt was still in Warren's car down in the garage, waiting to hear whether he would be needed. Logan had decided he was of more use scouting around for threats—the old lone-wolf instinct in him, rearing its head again. Probably he was sniffing around for the

Brotherhood, seeing whether he could pick any of them out of the crowd.

Everyone, including cameramen trained to identify celebrity faces, recognized Warren. His combination of looks, money, profile, and wings had made him one of the most recognizable people in the country—not that he cared, or would admit to caring. Camera crews shifted their positions so they could cover both Warren and the hearing floor. A TV reporter came over and shoved a microphone in his face.

"No availabilities right now," Warren said with a disarming smile. "Maybe after the business here is concluded. We're just here to watch, like everyone else."

Like everyone else, Ororo thought. Except we have knowledge the rest of you do not have. How many of the people in the gallery would cheer at the idea of a mutant-free future? More than would take action to prevent it, she knew that. Senator Kelly was more or less a decent human being, but he was driven by fear, and people driven by fear made poor choices. In a world where mutants were outnumbered at least a thousand to one, the poor choices of frightened nonmutants could have devastating, unintended consequences.

Sometimes Ororo believed that perhaps the X-Men did not listen enough to Magneto. Agree, no; listen, yes. Mutants should not try to conquer nonmutants, but there were certainly times when they did not do enough to advocate on their own behalf.

They were counting on Xavier to do exactly that. They always counted on him. If he could not defend them, they would be doomed to a pariah status—and that would lead to the murderous dystopia Kate had described to them that morning.

Ororo saw Xavier glance away from Kelly's oration, turning in her direction as if he had heard her thinking about him. Then she felt his touch, gentle but firm, in her mind. *Ororo. All is well in New Mexico? Your anxiety preceded you into the room.*

There have been urgent developments since

last we spoke, Professor. It would take some time to summarize.

Open your mind to me, then. Permit me your experiences. A moment is all that will be required.

Ororo did not like letting anyone into her mind, even Xavier, but she could see no better way to get across the urgency of the situation. *Yes,* she said.

She felt Xavier's presence, briefly but long enough to thoroughly unsettle both her mind and her stomach. Then he withdrew, leaving behind a lingering sense of shock, apprehension, and curiosity. Ororo looked to her left, where Kitty was sitting between her and Peter. Warren was on her other side, placed so he would be in the foreground of most camera angles.

Kitty's—Kate's—eyes widened and the muscles around her mouth tensed as Xavier announced himself inside her mind. A moment later, she looked around reflexively—the way a non-telepath almost always did when a telepath withdrew, as if the brain could not process the absence without relating it to a person nearby.

Kate reached over and took Ororo's hand. Ororo leaned in. "He won't hurt you. You know that."

She nodded. "This is where it's all going to happen, though. And I don't know how well my body—this body—is trained, what it can do...I hope I'm up to whatever is required of me." Then she leaned even closer. "Also, this is driving me crazy. I haven't told Peter yet that we're married in the future. Every time I look at him, I get a terrible pang, like I'm never going to see my Peter again."

"Shh," Ororo said—not to silence Kate, but to soothe her.

Xavier's mind alit on hers again. *Kitty believes her story,* he said. *And I can find no sign that she has been manipulated into telling it.*

"Some of your X-Men are in fact present at this hearing, are they not?" Senator Kelly was saying. Ororo looked around the room, wondering from which direction the attack would come. Capitol police officers were everywhere; she imagined there to be a significant undercover Secret Service presence, as well.

Any one of them might have been Mystique. To make matters worse, she did not know who else Mystique might have recruited to her new iteration of the Brotherhood—other than the Blob, who was certainly not in the room.

Xavier should have been able to find Mystique, though—and he had said nothing about detecting her presence. Had she hidden herself from his mental probes somehow, or had she changed her plan?

Or had the psychic projection of Kate Rasputin back in time disrupted this timeline already, setting off consequences for which they could not plan? Once time travel was injected into a situation, everything else became maddeningly uncertain.

"They are," Xavier said. "I see four of them: Piotr Rasputin, Katherine Pryde, Ororo Munroe, and Warren Worthington."

"Better known as…" Kelly made a production of consulting his notes and holding up pictures of each X-Man in costume as he continued. "Colossus! Sprite! Storm! And Angel! Mighty names. Where do the names come from, anyway?"

"The group assigns each other code names. As I imagine most groups do, whatever the genetic quirks of their members."

Kelly smiled. "Of course. I do hope, Professor Xavier, that their group presence is not intended as a show of…strength, perhaps?"

"They are here—as I am—to speak clearly on behalf of a population that is often misunderstood—and regrettably also often demonized," Xavier said.

At the same time, in Ororo's mind, he asked: *Do you believe her?*

I do.

As do I. Be prepared, Ororo. I fear no attack on myself, but if Senator Kelly dies today— demagogue though he may be—that bleak future Kate remembers may well come to pass.

Kelly had moved on. "Doctor MacTaggert."

"Yes, Senator Kelly. Please. Explain to me the need for these hearings, because frankly I cannot see it."

Ororo saw what she was doing, playing the aggressive role to make Xavier seem yet more reasonable and sympathetic. "The need," Senator Kelly answered, "is simple." He turned to the gallery, squaring his shoulders toward the anti-mutant protesters. "I merely wonder if—in a world of beings like Doctor Doom, like Magneto, like the Fantastic Four…these names! The Avengers! In such a world, with these and God knows how many others like them…I merely wonder if there's any place left for ordinary men and women."

"Of course there is," Moira said. "There is room for anyone who wishes to abide by the rules of our collective civil society."

"Yes," Kelly said, striking a thoughtful pose. "I wonder if the first Cro-Magnon said something similar to the last Neanderthal?"

Ororo. Kate is utterly certain of herself and her recent memories...let us say they bear out her story. We must act as if her information is correct and prepare for a Brotherhood attack.

She rose, and the others rose with her, following her up the aisle and out into the lobby. "Warren, are Kurt and Logan still in your car?"

"Last I knew," he said. "But when did I ever tell either one of them where to go?"

"Kitty, go and bring them in," Storm said. "Now."

WHAT a fascinating and inflammatory question, Senator," Moira said.

Kelly's smile grew just the slightest bit more predatory. "Inflammatory? The presence of costumed vigilantes in our midst—who can fly or turn to steel, who look like blue demons or clawed monsters—that's not inflammatory? It has certainly inflamed the good people of the gallery, who have turned out in such numbers to express their uncertainties. Which, Doctor MacTaggert, are my uncertainties as well."

He paused. "Professor Xavier, where have your X-Men gone? Are they afraid of a little public scrutiny?"

"Perhaps," Xavier said with a tight smile, "they were called away to fulfill an important task."

"No more mutants!" someone yelled from the gallery. Others picked it up, and it grew into a chant of more than a hundred people. Kelly looked around, half-heartedly gesturing for the committee chair to gavel the proceedings back to order. Cameras pushed in on him. NO MORE MUTANTS. NO MORE MUTANTS.

Kelly was trying not to smile.

People in the gallery started to stomp their feet. The balconies thumped and rocked. Even those not close to the anti-mutant protesters looked around, some up at the ceiling, as the vibrations grew stronger. Senate bailiffs and Capitol police made their way to the protesters, motioning for silence.

Meanwhile, TV cameras drank it all in and sent it out on a thousand feeds to millions of people. The feeds grew jerky as the shaking from the gallery increased. Throughout the hearing chamber, the faces of senators and spectators alike grew fearful as they started to realize that this much motion, this much noise, couldn't just be coming from people stomping their feet up in the balcony. This was something different.

As that thought took hold in the minds of everyone present, the vibration peaked. Cracks appeared along one wall of the hearing chamber. "Get out of here, everyone! Run!" a Capitol policeman shouted.

Then the wall collapsed. The sound of it boomed through the chamber, punctuated by the screams of spectators and those injured by flying debris. Sunlight flooded in, briefly blinding most of those present—except the senators themselves and Xavier and MacTaggert. They had been under the glare of TV lights, so their eyes to adjusted quickly to the sight of five figures standing in the rubble of the collapse.

"You will forgive the interruption, Senator

Kelly," said the figure in the center. The cameras loved her: tight white dress over athletic
curves, red hair setting off deep blue skin. "But
I found your question particularly apt, for we
all know what the first Cro-Magnons did to the
last Neanderthals."

She stepped forward, basking in the panic
as hundreds of spectators—including the protesters, scrambling to get off the balcony before
it collapsed—trampled each other on their way
to the doors. "I am Mystique!" she announced.
"My colleagues and I comprise the Brotherhood
of Mutants. We are your future, humans. Resist
us at your peril."

Mystique! The name went out to the millions—forever to be associated with the rumble
of the collapsed wall, the screams of the injured
and afraid, the shocked senators gaping from
behind their table in a swirl of dust. And flank-
ing her: Avalanche in his gauntlets and helmet,
Pyro like ambulatory flame in his red-and-yel-
low suit, Blob in his black wrestler's singlet.

And the silent Destiny, caped in blue, her eyes hidden as though her visions of the future must blind her to the present. No one who witnessed that moment would ever forget it.

"You been babblin' a lot about the mutant menace, Kelly," Blob said. Mystique shot him a look, but he ignored it and shoved his way forward through the rubble into the hearing chamber proper. "We're here to teach ya the error of your ways."

"You're hearing from the Blob," Mystique said. "In his unrefined way, he speaks for all of us. He is the immovable object, symbolizing the strength of our resolve. We have also brought to you Avalanche. Show them what you can do!"

Avalanche pointed at the marble floor; it crumbled to powder around Kelly's feet, leaving him trapped on a single tile with the beams of the floor exposed for twenty feet on three sides around him.

Before the crowd and the cameras could assimilate what had happened, Mystique went on.

She didn't want to give them a chance to get their breath. The more off-balance they were, the greater an impression the Brotherhood would leave—even before their final act: the public execution of Senator Robert Kelly. "Pyro!" she cried out like a circus ringmaster.

Pyro, with a malevolent wink, snapped his fingers. Gouts of fire shot from the portable spotlights set up for the television crews. The fires grew and intertwined, becoming a great flaming eagle that soared and floated out over the gallery.

"From England, a salute to the symbol of America," he said. The eagle crackled over the spectators. More of them fled. On the floor, Professor Xavier backed his wheelchair carefully away from the cracked and unstable edge of the hole Avalanche had opened in the floor.

"You see, Senator Kelly was correct," Mystique said. "We do have abilities and powers that you can never have. You should be afraid of us, because for centuries you have hunted and oppressed and vilified us. You have murdered us when you could. I myself have lost children because of human hate and fear.

"But now—from this moment forward— things will be very different. We are the Brotherhood of Mutants and we will not be cowed!"

Kelly, stunned like everyone else by the Brotherhood's violent appearance, at last recovered his composure. "This…is… monstrous!" he shouted over the din. "How dare you freaks turn the United States Senate into a battlefield!" He started to step toward Mystique, but halted at the edge of his small island in the middle of the disintegrated floor. "How dare you threaten me?! Marshals, arrest those…people!"

Blob laughed. "Kelly, you're either the bravest man here or the dumbest. Either way, you're gonna die today."

"That's enough out of you, fatso," said a Senate marshal who had worked his way around the rubble at the edge of the Brotherhood's entry hole. He put a hand on Blob's arm. "You and your mutie playmates have gone too far this time. You're under arrest!"

Blob looked at the hand on his forearm, and then at the marshal. His eyes narrowed. "Chump, you're talkin' to the Blob!" he said, and he backhanded the marshal hard enough to send him pinwheeling out over the hole in the floor, halfway to Kelly's island. The marshal's limp body caught for a moment on one of the exposed beams and then fell out of sight.

"I didn't get a chance to show what I could do for the cameras yet," he said, "but here's the short version. Nothing moves me if I don't wanna be moved, and there ain't a force on Earth that can hurt me. Anybody else wanna test me?"

There were several other marshals and Capitol police officers in the chamber, making sure civilians got out the public entrances. More had appeared behind the Senators' table, escorting the stunned Senators out and trying to reach Kelly. "Never mind me," he shouted. "Get them out of here and into jail! For good!"

The Brotherhood, as one, stepped into the chamber. "Jail?" Blob repeated. "I just got out. And I ain't goin' back."

"No media members will be harmed as long as their cameras keep recording," Mystique announced. "The Brotherhood wishes everyone to see this."

"See you murder me?" Kelly challenged. "You're proud of that?"

"I will be when it's done," Mystique said. "But since we are going to have the last word, I'll let you have your say now. Speak to the American people. Tell them again how mutants are to be hated and feared, and how we must be separated from everyone else. Perhaps herded into camps and exterminated. That's what you really want, isn't it, Senator Kelly? Go on. Tell them."

"They've already seen what they need to see. You're proving me right. If you're going to kill me, get on with it. History will show you for the craven murderers you are."

"History," said Mystique, "is written by the

winners, is it not? From now on, mutants will tell their own story and control their own destiny. Die now, and your hate-mongering will start to die with you." She nodded to Pyro. "Will you do the honors?"

"With pleasure," Pyro said. "But perhaps an American should strike this symbolic blow? Seems only proper."

"Everybody quit jawin'," Blob said. "I'll do it."

That was when the lightning struck.

CHAPTER 12

THEY split up as discussed. Wolverine planned to lead Storm and half of the FCA soldiers another block ahead to wrap around to the south on Fifth Avenue and approach the Baxter Building along 42nd Street. The rest of the FCA soldiers—including Rick—stayed with Peter, Kate, and the rapidly failing Rachel.

"I can't keep this up much longer," Rachel said.

"You must," Peter answered. "Hang on a little while yet, Rachel. There are more sacrifices to be made today."

"Franklin," she said, her voice barely above a whisper.

"Yes, Franklin. He died for this. Perhaps you will, too. But not yet, Rachel. Not yet. We still need you."

Peter carried her through the last stretch of the tunnel. Then they broke through a maintenance door into a parallel track that, according to Logan, would lead them to a subway-station entrance directly across the street from the Baxter Building's main lobby. They had all gone over what they remembered of the building's layout, knowing that the Sentinels would likely have rebuilt it to accommodate their size. Even so, they figured that the upper floors would still be laboratory and control space, because one of the Baxter Building's primary functions was to coordinate communications among all Sentinels along the Eastern seaboard. The Sentinels had commandeered the great skyscrapers of other cities, as well—Chicago, Atlanta, Houston, Los Angeles—and they maintained a signal booster at the top of One World Trade Center, but the Baxter Building was their nerve center. There, they had put the Fantastic Four's cutting-edge technology to work for their own genocidal ends.

And there, the X-Men were determined to

strike the decisive blow. If they failed, tomorrow would see a rain of warheads over North America. And if that did not stop the Sentinels, would other warheads then fall over London, Berlin, Moscow, Shanghai, Tokyo...?

Where would it end?

It wouldn't. Humanity would nuke itself out of existence.

"Rachel," Peter said.

She stirred and opened her eyes. "I'm still here," she said. "But I can feel myself coming apart, Peter. I can't—"

"Yes, you can." He set her down gently at the station entrance.

Kitty watched him and could understand why she had fallen in love with him. *Would* fall in love with him. How was her adult self coping with seeing Peter, knowing what their past was together—well, her past, and his future? It was a torment for all of them. She had to get back to her time so everything would be restored to its normal state. But what if adult-Kate succeeded?

Would that undo this future? What else would it undo? How many future lives would be saved, and how many lost?

These were not the kinds of questions a thirteen-year-old rookie member of the X-Men could handle. Kitty had to focus on what was in front of her: this future. This horrible future, teetering on the edge of nuclear apocalypse. Whatever Kate Pryde might do back in the past, surely the future her actions spawned couldn't be worse than this.

Framing the situation that way made her feel better. At least a little.

"Here is the danger," Peter said. "You cannot communicate with us actively, Rachel. That will bring the Sentinels down on you and Kitty."

"Me?" Kitty said. "I'm going in with you."

"Absolutely not," Peter said. "You must be here when the time comes for Rachel to send you back."

"And when is that time, exactly?" Kitty asked. "I can fight until then. You saw what I did. I can hurt them. I'm part of the team."

"Without a doubt, yes," Peter said.

"Then I should fight."

"If Sentinels approach you here, fight. If not, stay with Rachel. She should not be alone."

"Oh, stop it," Rachel said. "I'm going to die, Peter. It doesn't matter if anyone's here when it happens."

"Can you send this Kitten back to her time if she is phasing through the frame of the Baxter Building?" Peter asked. Rachel said nothing. "I thought not. You must stay here, Kitty, if we are to have any hope of returning you to your time."

He stood up. Across the intersection of Madison Avenue and 42nd Street, a Sentinel stood guard at the entrance to the Baxter Building. "It is almost three o'clock," Peter said. "Time to go."

PETER walked across Madison to the corner across from the entrance lobby, waiting for the signal that Storm and Logan were in place. Other Sentinels were visible patrolling near Grand Central and farther away to both north and south. Their escape had provoked a full-scale search operation, but the Sentinels would not anticipate a strike at the Baxter Building any more than an elephant anticipates a mouse going for its jugular. Peter had once read that elephants were frightened of mice because of the possibility that a mouse could run into the elephant's trunk. That would be a nuisance. But if a mouse got *stuck* in the elephant's trunk—that could be a real problem.

The X-Men hoped to stick a mouse up the elephant's trunk. At the Sentinel nerve center, they planned to clog up the communications and surveillance equipment that allowed the Sentinel-elephant to breathe. If it worked, the great beast would come crashing to earth. If not, mutantkind would be crushed under its invincible mass—and all of North America along with them.

Peter steeled himself, but only mentally. He reserved his physical transformation for later—for the inevitability of killing. He hated nothing more, but his principles were irrelevant given the stakes. If he had to kill, he would.

Across the street, FCA soldiers were leaning against the 42nd Street side of the Baxter Building's ground floor, telling jokes and pretending to be ordinary loiterers. They, too, were awaiting the signal from Logan and Storm. Then all proverbial hell would break loose.

Perhaps some of them would survive it.

More important, perhaps a future would survive *them*.

At three o'clock exactly, Peter looked up into the sky. He saw a bolt of lightning lance down, forking above the Baxter Building. One branch struck the cluster of antennae and satellite dishes on the building's roof. The other flashed down to ground level, striking the Sentinel at the lobby door and arcing out from it to every conductive structure nearby.

Sparks blasted out from the metal door frames. Diminishing fingers of electricity played around the street signs and other metal objects along the curb. When they dissipated, the Sentinel sat slumped against the wall, head down, smoke drifting from its eyes and other seams in its armor.

This time, Storm had had time to prepare.

Transforming into his organic-steel form, Peter ran north, catching up with Rick and his FCA comrades. "They'll know we're here now," he said as they got to the lobby doors. He shattered the heavy glass and led the FCA group through the lobby to a private elevator in the building's interior. Once, it had been reserved for the Fantastic Four; in the years since their deaths, it had sat unused.

"This one's yours," Peter said to Rick.

Rick stepped forward with a small object that looked like a flashlight. He activated it and shone its beam directly on a scanner next to the elevator door. Logan and the FCA had researched the building exhaustively and learned that the elevator was keyed to respond to a certain emergency code available to the Fantastic Four's close allies. They had then tracked down the code in a destroyed S.H.I.E.L.D. laboratory on Long Island and programmed it into this device. Now they held their collective breath, waiting to see whether the elevator was still functional. If not, it would be a long climb up the stairs, and the Sentinels would have plenty of time to prepare for their arrival.

The elevator doors opened, and Peter breathed a sigh of relief. So much had gone wrong already, it was a welcome change of pace to have a gamble pay off. He and the six FCA soldiers got on the elevator, and Peter hit the button for the top floor. The doors slid shut. For thirty-five floors, all they could do was wait.

PRETTY good show, 'Ro," Logan commented.

They stood watching the aftereffects of the lightning strike on the roof. Electrical components in the satellite dishes smoked and spat. Some of the antennae had toppled over the edge of the roof. A control station and transformer had exploded when the lightning hit, and it burned brightly.

Every Sentinel within twenty miles would know the Baxter Building was under attack. That was fine with Logan. By the time reinforcements arrived, he and Storm would either have finished the job, or they'd be finished themselves.

"Only the beginning, Logan," Ororo said. "Let's get moving. We don't want to leave Peter on his own."

She closed her eyes briefly and generated a field of static electricity, jamming any electronic detection and surveillance systems that had survived her first attack. The Sentinels already knew the X-Men were here, but the static field might keep them from zeroing in on the mutants' specific locations. Emphasis on *might*, she thought—and decided to create more fields, in different parts of the building. She drew the current along the length of the building's primary lightning rod, and from there into the outermost girders that ran straight down into its basement levels. Any observer sensitive to electromagnetism would register its presence. With luck, the

Sentinels would respond to it, dividing their attention and leaving an opening for the X-Men to infiltrate the control room.

Logan watched her until she nodded at him, indicating that the field was up. His claws flashed in the firelight as he cut through the chain on the roof-access door. It squealed on rusty hinges, but it opened, and he led Ororo to the fire stairs several floors down. They passed through an emergency door that led to a hall running along the edge of the building, connecting the freight-elevator shaft to Reed Richards' former lab space. Logan remembered coming here, a long time ago. He could almost hear Reed bossing everyone around, irritating Logan by being the smartest person in the room.

This was the simple part of the plan. The Sentinels knew they were coming, so there was no point in being coy. On the other hand, the Sentinels didn't know exactly where they were, because Storm had fried the Baxter Building's main electrical system. Any security cameras would be out of commission—but the main communications-control systems would have their own power source, insulated from electrical shocks to the building. So the next step was to hit that control room, hard and fast.

"Okay," Logan said. "If we got this figured right, the control room's on the other side of this door. They're gonna know we're around here somewhere, but one good thing about not being twenty feet tall is we can go lots of places in the building they can't. That's our only advantage. Soon as we're in the control room, it's gone."

"Then let's do some damage out here, eh?" Rick suggested.

The private elevator at the far end of the hall pinged. Its doors slid open to reveal Peter and the rest of the FCA.

"Boys and girls," Logan said. "New wrinkle in the plan. The three of us will hit the control room and take out as many of the Sentinels in there as we can, along with whatever's controlling their comm network. Meanwhile, the Free

Canadian Army goes on a little search-and-destroy through the rest of the building. Any electrical stuff, you blow it up. Anything more technologically advanced than a pencil, you shoot it. Stay out of areas where the Sentinels can get around easily."

"Yippee-kay-ay," Rick said. "Let's do it. We got at least a dozen shaped charges left. C4 solves lots of problems."

"Take it floor by floor, but keep moving downward," Logan said. "For all we know, the building's gonna come down at some point. You're gonna want to get out as soon as you can, but do some damage along the way."

"That's our specialty," said the medic who had treated Rachel.

"There's a fire staircase, back through the emergency door," Logan said.

"FCA, we are leaving," Rick said. He extended a hand. "Get out alive, Logan. We need you around."

"You too, bub," Logan said, shaking Rick's hand.

The three X-Men waited until the FCA soldiers were all gone down the fire stairs. "If we wait until they detonate their first charge, we might catch the Sentinels in a moment of distraction," Ororo said.

"Could be," Logan said. "I still feel like a mouse planning to take out the local cat."

"Funny you should say that. I was just thinking about mice, as well," Peter said. "But the context was elephants."

"We can go with that," Logan said. "Let's go scare us some elephants."

They followed the hall through a couple of turns. Then Logan said, "This is the door. I can hear them in there."

They waited.

OUTSIDE in the street, Kitty couldn't contain her impatience. "Nothing's happening," she said.

Rachel then did something that shocked her. She reached out to take Kitty's hand and squeeze it. Her grip was feeble, but the gesture sent a wave of emotion through Kitty she couldn't quite identify. "Give it a minute," Rachel said. "Won't be long."

A minute, thought Kitty. Strange to think a minute could be so important: the difference between waiting and doing, between living and dying. She had traveled twenty-two years into the future, and she might never get that time back. Every minute was important. How many old sayings were there about living every minute like it was your last? She'd dismissed them as the kind of thing older people said because they were jealous of the young, but she'd been wrong to do that. The Hellfire Club mercenaries could have ended her life in New Mexico. A Sentinel could have done the same here in New York. At any moment, all those infinite minutes and possibilities could be reduced to the cold certainty of death.

As they were about to be for Rachel. Kitty looked at her, watched her life force slowly ebbing away. Rachel did not cry out, did not visibly fight. But Kitty could see the intensity of her struggle in the tautness of her facial muscles, in the slow care she took with every word she spoke, every motion of her body. To Rachel, every minute *was* now precious, because she had so few left.

God, to know you were going to die…

But didn't Kitty know that, too? Her chances of getting back to her own time were—well, maybe not zero, but not good, either. It was much more likely that a Sentinel would vaporize or crush her here in the future. And more likely still that Rachel's resolute struggle to hold her body together would fail before she could swap Kitty and her older self back to their proper places again.

Kitty understood they needed to wait as long as possible, giving her older self maximum time to avert the assassination of Senator Kelly—assuming time passed at the same relative rate in both her past and this present/future. The truth was, she might return in the blink of an eye, considered from her past self's point of view—and that would create another future. Or she might return after exactly as much time as she had experienced here, in which case it was possible that the line from that past to this future would be unbroken. Kitty's head spun a little thinking about it. She was smart, and knew it, but anyone who thought hard about relativity without a little bit of dizzy wonder wasn't doing it right.

Either way, to be safe, she needed to wait as long as possible here—which meant, basically, as long as Rachel had the strength to return her. Unless there was another way back, and Kitty doubted that very much.

Boiling the situation down to its essence, Kitty Pryde knew she was probably going to die very soon, and she was terrified.

But all she could do was wait a minute, as Rachel had said. Wait, and hope, and then take action when the time came.

FIVE minutes later, a thump and rumble shook the floor. "That's it," Logan said.

He tested the door latch. It was locked. With one claw, he cut through the bolt holding it shut and eased the door open enough for the three of them to get a look inside.

They were on the floor of the control room, which appeared to occupy the entirety of the building's footprint except for the narrow hallway and elevator shafts. The ceiling was maybe fifty feet above them, and a catwalk ran around three sides of the room about halfway up the walls.

In the center of the space stood a shining metal column, laced with fiber-optic cable and shimmering behind a force field of some kind. Whether it was a protective measure or a containment protocol, they didn't know. And it didn't much matter. The column had to come down if they were going to do more than scrap a few Sentinels.

"That'll be it," Logan whispered.

There were whole banks of terminal screens

and workstations, scaled to the Sentinels' size. At one of them stood a Sentinel, tracing lines on a touch screen. "Omega-class," Storm whispered. They stood out from the ordinary Sentinels by virtue of the identification numbers stamped into their armor. The lower the number and fewer the digits, the higher the Sentinels' rank and ability. Normal Sentinels were fierce enemies; Omega-class Sentinels were more than strong enough to kill all three X-Men if they didn't do something to tilt the odds in their favor.

"You got another Fastball Special in you, Petey?" Wolverine asked. "I'll open this bastard up before he knows we're here. Might not kill him, but it'll sure slow him down. Then you and 'Roro finish him off."

"There will be others," Storm said. "In fact, I can see one up on the catwalk. It is facing away from us."

"One thing at a time," Logan said.

Peter crouched and Logan stepped into his hand, bracing himself against Peter's shoulder.

Peter heaved Wolverine through the air toward the Sentinel, the *snikt* of Logan's claws sounding sharply against the hum of the force field and the ambient whir of cooling fans.

Logan was moving at something close to a hundred miles per hour, and he had perhaps twenty-five yards to cover before hitting the Sentinel. That left the Sentinel approximately a half-second to respond. But in addition to superior armaments, the Omega-class Sentinels had enhanced sensory mechanisms and reflex arrays. Almost faster than the human eye could follow, the Sentinel spun, raised a hand, and blasted Logan out of the air with an energy beam emanating from its palm.

An afterimage of that moment would remain burned into Peter's mind as long as he lived: Logan's body arching in the Sentinel's beam. The gruesome contrast between the parts of Logan's body outside the beam's cone, charring and melting, and the almost X-ray clarity of his Adamantium skeleton in the brilliant light. The sound of Logan's feral dying shriek cutting off as his lungs and vocal cords vaporized.

Of all of them, Peter realized, he had never really imagined Logan could die.

The stink of burned flesh and hair flooded the room as Logan's body crashed into the catwalk over the control-room door. He tumbled down to land in a smoking, charred heap in front of Peter and Ororo.

"Pathetic organic being," the Sentinel said. "Did you imagine you could approach—much less penetrate—this facility without being detected?"

Apparently, the other thing that set the Omega-class Sentinels apart from their subordinates was that they had been programmed to be arrogant.

"Mutants 049 and 116, you are still of some use to us. Yield immediately and survive."

Storm's answer was a blast of lightning.

The intensity of the electrical fields present in the control room gave her a huge reservoir of energy to tap. She linked it to her weather powers, amplifying them beyond anything she had ever before attempted. Earlier that night, caught by surprise, she had been unable to bring down Sentinels. Now, with this virtually limitless ambient energy field at her command, she hit the Omega-class Sentinel with a jagged blast that slagged its internal circuitry and left a smoking, fused hole just above and to the left of its torso repulsor lens.

Feelers of lightning licked out from the Sentinel. Some were absorbed into the force field; others flashed across the surfaces of the control panels lining the walls. They flickered and sparked, but the system as a whole was undamaged.

Logan lay silent, much of his flesh burned away from the Adamantium rods and casings that reinforced his skeleton. His upper body had taken the brunt of the blast. His ribcage and collarbones were exposed, along with the entirety of one arm's bones. His other arm, the right, was bare Adamantium down to the elbow; the hand below it twitched, its claws flicking irregularly out and back in. From the waist down, the damage was more superficial: third-degree burns that had charred him down to the muscle tissue. His face, too, was partially burned away, exposing his Adamantium jaw and the lower half of the skull. One of his eyes was gone. The other stared sightlessly off to one side, where the Sentinel toppled to the floor with a thud that echoed throughout the room.

The Sentinel on the catwalk said, "Mutant infiltration of control room. Request reinforcements."

It rose up, away from the catwalk, and faced Storm across the smoky width of the room. "One mutant terminated," it said. "Two hostile. Location of others unknown."

Another distant boom shook the building. The Free Canadian Army was doing its job, Storm thought. Time to keep on doing hers.

Peter charged out from under the catwalk overhang, leaping over the body of his friend to grab onto one of the hovering Sentinels' feet. The exhaust from its boot rocket seared him, but he did not feel it. The Sentinel, its balance upset by the sudden addition of five hundred pounds to one leg, swung and dipped in the air. Peter held on to it with one arm wrapped around its ankle and kicked his legs out, hooking his own ankles around the catwalk railing. The railing was constructed of heavy steel vertical beams connected by braided steel cables the thickness of a normal human arm.

With his legs scissored around one of those beams, Peter jackknifed his body—driving the Sentinel down and playing a devastating game of crack-the-whip with its head, which struck the control-room floor hard enough to shake the walls and bounce Logan's remains into the air. Bits of the Sentinel's cranial armor flew off to bang and clatter across the floor as Logan's body hit the ground again.

Across the room, a door slid open. Through it Peter saw two more Sentinels, both Omega-class. Electronic gibberish was pouring from the prone Sentinel's damaged head. It tried to get up, but its hard landing had apparently damaged its inertial-control and balance systems.

"Finish it, Ororo!" Peter shouted. "I will take these!"

He felt static electricity begin to play across his steel skin as Ororo gathered energy. Peter raced along the catwalk, changing the Sentinels' angle of fire. They both discharged palm energy beams at him, and both missed—but one of the beams severed the cables along the catwalk, destabilizing part of it. Peter lost his balance and pitched over the catwalk's edge, catching the closest beam and hanging over thirty feet of empty space.

Ororo saw this and changed her plan. The prone Sentinel was still scrabbling on the floor, squawking incomprehensibly. It was much less of a threat than the two converging on Peter.

Wind rose in the room, and the temperature began to fall. One of the Sentinels charged toward Ororo; the other reached both hands up to catch the dangling Peter. She would only have time to strike at one of them. She felt the energy exchange inside her body as she forced the heat from the room, creating a zone of intense cold around her, and prepared to focus it—on one Sentinel or the other.

Peter swung himself up, seeing the oncoming Sentinel reaching for his legs. He felt the wave of cold roll through the room and looked to Ororo, who was hidden behind a shield of ice. Then he looked down. The Sentinel that had targeted him was rimed with frost, its armor cracking under the molecular pressures of a sudden two-hundred-degree temperature change.

The other Sentinel swung a fist and shattered the ice shield, knocking Ororo out of the air in the same sweeping motion. The shield absorbed much of the blow's force, but Storm hit the floor hard and tumbled. The Sentinel stepped closer, opening its hands. Its palms began to glow as its energy beams charged.

Peter found his feet and ran along the catwalk toward Storm. He held the end of the severed cable, popping it out of its fixtures as he ran.

Neither of them saw Logan's remains start to move.

CHAPTER 13

EVERY feed coming from the Senate hearing room whited out momentarily as a lightning bolt—from a clear blue sky!—struck the floor at Blob's feet. He reeled back, along with the other four members of the Brotherhood. When the glare faded, five figures stood opposing the Brotherhood. These were names recently heard in the Senate: Storm in the middle, with Colossus, Wolverine, Angel, and Kitty/Kate Pryde arrayed around her in a loose half-circle.

"If you mean to harm Senator Kelly, or anyone here, you'll have to go through us," Storm said, her voice ringing through the chaos.

Mystique smiled, and her empty eyes flashed. "That will be a distinct pleasure." She pointed at Storm first, then flung her arms wide to encompass the entire chamber. "Kill them!"

The few spectators who had remained in their gallery seats, stunned by the spectacle of the Brotherhood's entrance, jumped up and ran. Police officers stayed long enough to make sure everyone else got out, and then they were gone, too.

Of the senators, only Kelly remained, on his marble isthmus projecting out over the empty space where most of the rest of the floor had been. A step forward, left or right, and Kelly would topple into the building's basement levels. Most of the reporters and camera crews were gone, too, except for a few who'd crammed themselves behind the senators' table, hoping they could get good footage and survive.

Playing to the cameras, Mystique let the other four Brotherhood members charge forward. "Senator Kelly is fond of speaking against the mutant menace," she proclaimed over the chaos of fleeing civilians and cascading rubble. "My colleagues and I are that menace incarnate! As an example of our power—as an object lesson to those who would oppose us—we intend to kill him!"

Avalanche struck first, thrusting both fists forward to create a shock wave that plowed the remaining floor up into marble shards, splintered beams, and plaster dust. The wave broke over the X-Men, toppling Wolverine and Colossus down into the exposed basement. Angel grabbed Kate, rising into the air and bearing her to safety beneath the balcony overhang on one of the few stable patches of floor. Storm, too, was in the air. Suspended below the gallery ceiling, she watched the rest of the X-Men struggle against the wave of debris.

Colossus and Wolverine had just dug themselves out of the pile of wreckage in the basement and climbed back into the gallery when Pyro caught Colossus in a clawed hand of animated fire. "Let's see what the melting point of your metal body is, Colossus!" Pyro said. The hand closed into a fist, searing Peter's body and setting smaller fires along the broken ends of beams and timbers jutting from the debris.

"That's a fancy flamethrower you're packing,

bub," Wolverine said. "Wonder what'll happen if I punch my claws through the fuel tank and into your *stinkin' hide!*" He lunged forward, his claws catching the firelight as they arced toward the tank on Pyro's back.

"Logan, no!" Storm commanded, landing on the floor and reaching out to stop him. But he wasn't listening. The fury of battle was upon him as surely as it had always come over men like him, dating back to the berserkers who fought in bear skins in the forests of Germania.

Everything, Storm knew, was going out via live feeds to the entire world. The reputation of all mutants was at stake here—not to mention their survival, if what Kate Pryde said was true. They absolutely could not be seen killing each other in the halls of the Senate. That was what the Brotherhood wanted, and it was also what the enemies of mutantkind wanted. Storm refused to give it to them.

She raised a pocket storm, a whirlwind of tornado intensity less than thirty feet across, and drew all the ambient moisture in the room straight into it. Logan, caught in mid-lunge, was thrown up and away from Pyro. "Storm, have you flipped?" he raged. "Whaddaya think you're doing?"

Saving all of us, she thought. Leading.

With Logan safely out of claw range, she flicked her fingers. The whirlwind's accumulated water sprayed out in a wave, drenching Pyro and Colossus and extinguishing the flame that held Peter in its grasp.

"Now you see, Senator Kelly," she said, loudly enough for the camera crews to pick up. "You tar all mutants with the same brush, but some of us will fight to save even our deadliest enemies."

"He's gone!" Kate Pryde said from above. Storm looked up and saw Kate hanging on to Angel. Then she looked out over the yawning hole in the floor to the small patch left intact when the Brotherhood had tried to isolate Kelly. The Brotherhood had not counted on the X-Men's opposition—but why not, since they had Destiny on their side?

Senator Kelly had indeed vanished. Ororo looked down into the basement. He was not visible there. He must have picked his way along the small path left to him and fled, she thought, taking advantage of the X-Men's protection.

Destiny was nowhere to be seen. Nor was Mystique. "Nice move, Storm," Angel commented. "Last thing we need is Logan carving someone up on live TV, even if it's a villain."

Infuriated by Storm's interruption, Pyro raised another stream of fire and sent it in a sweeping arc toward Angel. "One thinks of Icarus, does one not?" he called, laughing. Angel dodged the flames licking at his wingtips, but he had to let Kate go. Fire slashed through the space where she had been.

Kate Pryde fell. She landed as gracefully as could be expected on the intact part of the floor, in front of the senators' long table.

She looked across the scene. Angel was desperately dodging Pyro's fiery creations, trying to get close enough to incapacitate him. Avalanche deflected a clawed strike from Wolverine and answered with a tremor that lifted the floor under Logan's feet, pitching him up and back into a row of seats. Colossus and Blob were trading blows, but even Peter could not do much damage to the Blob.

The only positive so far was that no mutants had been killed on a worldwide newsfeed. But if she couldn't find Senator Kelly, it was only a matter of time. Kate hesitated. She could stay with her friends and fight to save their lives—or she could leave them to find Kelly and perhaps save the lives of every mutant in the world.

She thought of the cemetery in the South Bronx. She thought of her own children. There was really only one choice.

Kate Pryde ran—out through the open door that led into the private, secured areas of the Senate office building. If Mystique and Destiny were hunting Senator Kelly, as Kate suspected, she might already be too late. Thinking back, she remembered that the news reports of Kelly's assassination had not said precisely who killed him. An exhaustive investigation had failed to uncover critical details, likely because traditional forensics and police protocols were ill-equipped to deal with mutant powers. The actual killer could be any one of the Brotherhood.

Blob, Avalanche, and Pyro were in the hearing chamber, though. Destiny and Mystique were not, and neither was Senator Kelly. Kate would have to play the odds, long though they might be.

THE LOBBY of the Hart Building was as chaotic as the scene inside the hearing room, if less lethal. People screamed and shoved their way toward the exits, their panic bringing out the worst in them. Xavier could feel the intensity of their fear—and the way it decayed into anger and then into hate. Capitol police fought to keep order and make sure that the mass exodus didn't degenerate into a stampede.

Moira MacTaggert pushed Xavier's wheelchair along the wall, trying to stay away from the mob. If he were pitched out of his chair, he could be trampled. With the building shaking around them and the smell of smoke in the air, the majority of the fleeing spectators were headed for the closest door. But there was a second door at the far end of the lobby.

Xavier pointed toward the farther door, and Moira guided his chair that way. He guessed the extra time involved would be justified by the decreased probability that they would be swept up and injured by the mob.

There was also the possibility that one of the anti-mutant protesters would recognize them and choose this moment to make a violent statement. The more Moira and Xavier stayed out of the crowds and in better view of the police, the less likely that was to happen.

"Charles," she said, "you had that I'm-doing-telepathy look on your face right before all hell broke loose. What is happening?"

"It's almost too fantastic to believe," Xavier

said. He had to force himself to go on, knowing that Moira would not believe it at first—just as he had not. He chose his words carefully. "Apparently the mind and persona of the adult Kate Pryde, from twenty-two years in the future, has psychically exchanged places with her present-day self."

Moira stopped pushing the chair. Xavier knew she was looking at him, wondering whether he had suffered some injury she hadn't noticed. "Charles, that's daft," she said.

"I scanned her mind. It is the truth," Xavier said.

He reached out to touch the minds of his protégés still fighting in the hearing chamber. They radiated anger, fear, and resolve. The battle was not going well, but neither was it lost. If Kate Pryde was correct, Storm was doing the right thing by holding as many of the Brotherhood as possible in place while Senator Kelly got to safety. Alive, he was a bigot and a demagogue, but he would become a martyr if he died. That left the X-Men with two choices—both poor, but one demonstrably better than the other.

"Kate said that someone named Rachel Summers performed the projection back in time," Xavier said.

"Summers?" None of them knew of a Rachel Summers. "Charles, if this is…if time travel is possible and history is mutable, we'll have to redefine our concept of reality itself."

Leave it to an academic to theorize in the midst of a terrorist attack, Charles thought.

"We'll never be completely sure what…*is*… from one moment to the next," Moira went on. "Terrifying."

"Perhaps we never should have been sure," Xavier said. "God only knows what poor Kitty is experiencing in the future Kate described to me."

The crowd had shifted as more escapees from the hearing chamber packed into the lobby—some injured, most panicked. Moira had to stop and wait for a cluster of people to pass, carrying an unconscious man by his arms and legs. He was covered in dust and bleeding badly from a wound on his scalp.

"Professor Xavier," an approaching police officer said. She pointed toward a door that— if his memory served—led through the interior of the building to the other side, away from the wing currently in danger of collapse. "Let's get you and Doctor MacTaggert out of here."

A fine idea, Xavier thought. Particularly since he had heard a number of minds in the crowd register his name—and not in a positive fashion.

The officer opened a door and led them down a hall lined with doors. Some of them were open, revealing offices and meeting rooms. This was where the business of the Senate was really done, Charles reflected. Away from the cameras, in the quiet spaces where people could sit down, talk, and decide what they were willing to give up to achieve their goals.

"You'll be safe here," the officer said, opening a door to an unoccupied office. She reached for something on her belt—a ring of keys?

No, Charles thought. "Moira!" he said. "I sense some kind of energy field. This woman, she is not what she seems—*aarrgghh!*"

Moira jerked the wheelchair to a halt. The police officer turned, smiled, and discharged a spray of whitish-pink powder that coated both Xavier and Moira.

"You sensed the damper field that kept you from reading my mind, my dear distracted professor. Your worry for your little X-Men left you vulnerable." As the police officer spoke, her physical form shimmered and melted, revealing Mystique. "And now it is too late for your mental powers to do you any good."

Moira sagged, trying to hold on to the handles of Xavier's wheelchair. She slumped to the floor, eyes half-open and unfocused. Her breathing was barely detectable. Xavier's head slumped forward onto his chest.

"A little shot of nerve gas to paralyze you both," Mystique said. "But I wouldn't want to deprive you of the experience of hearing everything that goes on around you. Without your telepathic guidance, Storm and the X-Men will be crippled. We already had the advantage, Xavier. Now that advantage is decisive."

Destiny appeared from inside the office. "You ought to kill him while you have the chance," she said.

"He is of more use as a potential hostage," Mystique said. "We can always kill him later. I would prefer to learn whatever he has to tell us first, and then dispose of him after our business with Senator Kelly is concluded."

"Did you not just say, back in the suite, that we would kill these two in addition to Senator Kelly?"

"I did say that, and we still will," Mystique said. "But I prefer not to act when I have incomplete information. That's your role here. How fares our futur e?"

"It is as I told you before," Destiny said. "Beyond a certain point, the images become jumbled, difficult to read. There is a random factor present, an anomaly that strikes to the very heart of the timestream. So long as it exists, nothing is certain."

"Well, what is it? Locate it, and we will eliminate it."

Mystique wheeled Xavier's chair into the office, then returned to the hall to drag MacTaggert in, as well. This was Senator Kelly's office. He would return here sooner or later. Of that much she was certain.

"Its nature prevents me from identifying it," Destiny said. "It is not merely a new factor, around which other factors resettle themselves into predictable patterns. It is an uncertainty itself; while it exists, no certainty is possible."

Mystique slammed the door. "Well, what are you here for if not to reduce uncertainty?"

Unperturbed, Destiny said, "Would you rather not have known that this new element had been introduced? I can remain silent if you would prefer."

Mystique fumed for a moment. She contemplated killing Xavier and MacTaggert. It would make her feel better and prevent this conversation from ever leaving Senator Kelly's office. After brief consideration, however, she rejected the idea. In an uncertain situation, the prudent leader amassed potential resources. A dead Xavier was not a resource. A hostage Xavier who could be forced to yield secrets? That was a resource.

She and Destiny had a long history together. Mystique valued Destiny's advice, for obvious reasons. But she sometimes wondered whether she had made a strategic mistake allying herself so closely with someone who always knew what she was going to do next. A vexing question. Once the matter of Senator Kelly was settled, it might be worth re-thinking. One could not just throw away long friendships, of course—but neither could one let sentimentality become a fatal blind spot.

"Very well," she said, in a calmer tone. "It doesn't matter. With or without your foreseeing help, my friend, the Brotherhood will prevail."

IN THE hearing chamber, the battle raged. Not all of the bystanders had managed to escape yet, and neither had the more foolhardy news crews. Their lives were in Storm's hands. The entire building was going to come down with them in it, sooner rather than later, if she didn't do something.

So she did.

A wind rose inside the chamber, drawing air from outside through the entry hole blasted by the Brotherhood. Storm held it in a spiral, like the tiny whirlwind she had used on Logan, and let it grow more powerful. Pyro attempted to counter her by sending bolts of fire toward her, but Storm blew them out before they reached her. Avalanche tried, literally, to shake her focus—but she floated free of the ground, and his shock waves passed around her with no effect.

The wind tore seats loose, lifted tables to spin through the air, and shattered the windows that looked down from beyond the balcony. Growing desperate, Avalanche started to shake the building itself, hoping to collapse the entire structure around them. No, Storm thought, as the windstorm grew and concentrated itself. She held it away from the corner where the TV crews still huddled, allowing everything else in the room to become an irresistible vortex. When she had drawn the energy of a pocket hurricane into the confined space, she unleashed it on the intact wall facing the open expanse of the National Mall.

The wall exploded outward from the overpressure, as if a huge bomb had gone off with all of its force concentrated in only one direction. Storm allowed herself to be drawn along with the blast of wind. Around her tumbled Logan, Avalanche and Pyro. They hurtled in a loose group out across the grand steps at the front of the building and onto the manicured green of the Mall.

She saw all of them except the Blob and Colossus. Storm had been afraid of that. She had hoped to catch Blob by surprise, before he could root himself to the earth, but his response had been quicker than she'd anticipated. Even as she rode the whirlwind outside and tried to set her friends down more gently than her foes, Storm wondered what they could do if the Blob simply refused to be extracted from the building. He would tear it down out of spite, even if Senator Kelly escaped.

And speaking of Senator Kelly, where was he? Ororo had a feeling that if the Brotherhood had succeeded in killing him, they would be shouting that from the rooftops. So he was most likely alive, but she disliked not knowing where he might be—almost as much as she disliked not knowing where Kate had gotten to.

Were the two disappearances linked? Had Kate gone looking for Senator Kelly? Ororo could not break away from this fight to find out. Too many lives were at stake here.

Fire swirled along the wind currents, flaring out into the open air. "You see, Storm, your winds only feed my flames!" Pyro said.

Colossus was also still inside. He and Blob were no doubt locked together, and Storm feared that even Peter's prodigious strength might meet its match in the Blob.

But they had another, and perhaps more immediate, problem. As the dust and debris blew away, Storm saw that a military rapid-response team, complete with light armor, had already cordoned off the entire area around the Senate building. Their officers were pointing out the locations of all known mutants, apparently without regard to which side each mutant was fighting on. If the X-Men weren't careful, Ororo knew, they would find themselves under assault from the military even as they fought to save lives from the Brotherhood.

The only benefit of this military intervention was that it kept civilians away. They had all been evacuated to gawk from a safe distance. Ambulance lights strobed behind the military position as emergency workers treated the injured from the Brotherhood's initial attack. Washington, D.C., was as prepared as any city in the world to deal with an event of this nature.

Storm heard amplified voices shouting more orders, but could not make out what they were saying. Where were Moira, Professor Xavier, and Kate? Had they found Senator Kelly? She had not felt Xavier's touch on her mind since just after the battle had been joined.

Fight the battle you can fight, she told herself. It was her responsibility to lead the X-Men against the Brotherhood here, before more lives were lost.

BACK inside the destroyed hearing chamber, Blob held Colossus by the arm. Colossus unloaded a punch to his face, but the Blob just laughed.

"She couldn't make me go," he said. "Nobody makes Fred J. Dukes do something he don't want to do. And as long as I got hold of you, you don't go anywhere until I say so."

He paused, and a cruel leer exposed oddly perfect teeth in his homely face. "But maybe it's time for you to take a little ride."

CHAPTER 14

PETER was not going to get there in time. Half the expanse of the Baxter Building control room stretched between him and the Sentinel poised to burn Ororo to ashes. The glow of its palm beams brightened. It would fire at any moment. Desperately he ran, knowing he wouldn't make it. He might as well have been outside the building, or back on the farm in Siberia.

Logan was gone, soon Ororo would be, and how much longer after that could Peter survive? What would Kate find when she returned from the past—if she ever did? And if she did not, how long would poor Kitty survive in her adult body with Rachel dying at her side?

Things could hardly be worse, Peter thought. And then, at least for one fleeting moment, they got better.

Ororo had fallen near the original, human-sized door the three of them had used to enter the control room. The Sentinel stepped over the body of the one she'd destroyed, leaning close to her. "You are no longer useful," it said. "The time of mutants is over. Sentinel directives mandate elimination."

With its next step, it planted an immense booted foot next to the smoking, mangled remains of Wolverine—who lifted his head.

"Logan," Ororo said in amazement.

He reached up with one arm that was half flesh and half exposed Adamantium, and his claws punched into the back of the Sentinel's left heel. Logan jerked the claws sideways, severing the hydraulic assembly that maintained tension in the Sentinel's lower leg and therefore controlled its balance.

It swayed to its left, arms splaying out as its palm beams discharged. One of them blew a hole in the ceiling. The other scorched through the wall just in front of Peter as, with that same hand, the Sentinel grasped the catwalk for support.

That gave Colossus the extra moment he needed to reach the Sentinel. He dashed along the length of its arm and flipped a heavy cable around its neck. Then he pulled, slowly garrotting the Sentinel. He couldn't strangle it, obviously. But Peter knew if he pulled long enough and hard enough, eventually its head would come off. And in any case, he would keep it occupied so it couldn't target Storm.

At least until one of the two other, damaged Sentinels in the room recovered enough to kill them.

The Sentinel reeled back from Ororo, with Peter still hauling at the cable around its neck. She scrambled across the floor to Logan, then stopped as the staggering Sentinel stepped back and crushed Logan under its damaged heel. As quickly as the foot came down, it rose again. The Sentinel began thrashing its way across the room, but Ororo could see the damage it had done to Logan.

His Adamantium skeleton was undamaged,

of course, but his body was completely devastated. Only the invulnerability of his skull kept his face intact enough for him to speak. "'Ro?" he said. "Can't see."

Both of his eyes were gone.

"Tried to slow it down," he said.

"You did," she said. "You saved me one more time."

"Okay. Good. That's all I got," he said, and died. She saw the last life leave him. His hands relaxed; the points of his claws made small clinks as they settled onto the concrete floor, not even hard enough to leave a scratch.

Peter pulled on the cable with all the strength his anger could give him, bracing his feet against the metal flange that ringed the Sentinels' upper torso. He felt something give, and pulled harder. The Sentinel started to scream, an alarm sound that felt to Peter like a cry of pain and fear. Did the Sentinels feel fear? He did not know. What he knew was that *people* had felt fear, and the Sentinels were responsible. He flicked both wrists, wrapping the cable once more around them, and pulled again.

The Sentinel's head tore off in a shower of sparks and a gout of dark lubricant and hydraulic fluids. Peter fell, landing flat on his back; the Sentinel's head crashed down face-first beside him a moment later, splattering him with slick oils.

He looked over and saw Logan. Ororo stood over his body in a tearful rage. Peter could feel the energy radiating from her. She walked across the room—past the twitching Sentinel with its broken head; past the decapitated body of the Sentinel that had killed Logan; past the body of the first Sentinel, the hole punched through its torso still smoldering.

As she approached the frozen Sentinel, its armor crackled anew. Ororo drew the heat from it and from the air around it. Icy fog formed in the room, and nearby glass monitors shattered.

"Monsters," she said. "Not even monsters. Idiot machines, thinking you have reason. Murderous wind-up toys. You have almost killed us.

Almost. But we will die no more."

Long cracks appeared in the Sentinel's armor, and pieces of it began to shear away. Ororo hovered five or six feet in the air, lifted up from the floor by the intensity of the energies she channeled.

"Now, Peter!" Ororo cried out. Peter leaped forward, clenching both fists together.

The blow shook the floor as the Omega-class Sentinel seemed to detonate under him. Supercooled bits of it peppered the room, shattering what windows still remained and punching shrapnel holes in the banks of terminals and monitoring equipment that lined the walls. The force of the Sentinel's disintegration pitched Peter's quarter-ton mass most of the way back to Logan's body. He landed flat on his back and lay stunned for a moment, blinking.

The control room filled with mist as the pieces of the destroyed Sentinel's body rewarmed, and the ambient temperature climbed back toward freezing. Smoke hung in a layer high in the room. The hole in the ceiling acted as a chimney, drawing the warmer air up and out into the chilly night. Sparks fell in cascades from damaged machinery. It looked as though fires were burning outside.

Let the whole building burn, Peter thought. Except it wouldn't. The Sentinels would fight the fire and bring it under control.

Peter and Ororo had a moment, no more. Their primary objective still stood before them, that column of cables and steel protected behind the coruscating barrier of its force field. The core powering the Sentinels' North American surveillance matrix was still intact.

But not for long. With the Sentinel guards dispatched, the X-Men had bought a moment to determine how that force field worked. Surely there was a way to overload or bypass it, if they could find it in time. All they needed was to discover the weak point in the system.

Could it be that they were about to win? *Actually* win, not just fight a holding action that would delay their extinction for a few hours or a day? Peter had not imagined that possible during the process of the plan's hatching, debate, and execution. Nevertheless, he had supported the plan. Against his better judgment, he had allowed his wife's mind to be separated from her body and projected more than two decades back in time—with no idea whether he would ever see her again. Then the unexpected twist: young Kitty Pryde, the Sprite he remembered as a skittish girl, speaking to him out of Kate Rasputin's physical form. If he had known that would happen, would he have consented? It seemed one strangeness too far, a little too much to expect of any man.

But if all could be put right—if Rachel could keep herself alive long enough to restore past and present Kate/Kitty to their times—then it would all have been worth it.

If Kate had been able to divert the Brotherhood's attack on Senator Kelly. What was happening at this moment back in the past? Did that question even have any meaning? It had been four hours or so since the telepathic projection. During that time, had the X-Men come to believe Kate's story? Had they gotten to Washington, D.C.? Had they contacted Professor Xavier? What was happening, or had happened? Nothing here looked any different, of course, and probably never would. In all likelihood, they were fighting for a different future—one that none of them would ever experience.

Or would they? How much could they assume they knew about the workings of time? It was a heady question. Peter wondered, in the aftermath of smoke and freezing fog that was also preamble to the final act, whether they would ever know what Kate's actions in the past had accomplished. They had talked it over endlessly, speculating and arguing whether this future would be changed, or unmade, or left completely intact by the creation of a parallel new timeline. Would any of them ever know?

They had sacrificed Franklin and Logan, and soon Rachel, for the possibility that others might live. Nothing could be certain, maybe not even the past—and definitely not the future. If Kate was coming back, Peter wanted to be able to tell her they had succeeded. And above all, Kitty needed to return to the past, so she could fall in love with the younger version of him. They would make something beautiful together. If Kate's mission succeeded, even their children might survive.

He cut off that train of thought. He would need focus to survive the next few hours. All they had done was fire the first shot of the last battle, and they had lost half their number in doing so. There was no room to make any more mistakes.

All those thoughts and speculations flashed through Peter's mind in the time it took him to stand up and walk over to the core. He gazed at it, wondering how it worked. Advanced technology was not his specialty. He reached out and placed a hand on the force field.

An explosion reverberated through the building. Was the FCA still bombing their merry way down to the ground floor, or had the havoc in this room started some kind of chain reaction?

"Ororo," he said. "Should we try to overload this force field, or will it be faster to bypass it and try to destroy the control array's power source? There will be more Sentinels here soon."

RACHEL said something, just a little too quietly for Kitty to understand.

Kitty looked from the Baxter Building to her and then back up at the building. Smoke poured from its roof, and at least three fires glowed from different floors. "What, Rachel?" she asked.

"Doesn't matter," Rachel said.

The last of the FCA guerrillas burst out of the front entrance, followed seconds later by an explosion that blew out all the windows facing Madison Avenue and 42nd Street. The defeated Sentinel sitting against the wall fell over on to its side as the FCA followed Rick over to Kitty and Rachel.

"What's the word?" Rick asked.

"We don't know anything," Kitty said. "At

least I don't. What did you see in there?"

"We stayed in the old parts of the building. Sentinels didn't redo all of it. We peeked out of the fire staircase, blew all the electrical stuff we could find, and kept moving," Rick said. "That's what Logan said he wanted."

"You saw all of them inside?"

"Logan, Peter, Ororo. Were there more?" Rick asked. "That's all we saw. You guys were talking about someone else. Is he—?"

"That's all of them. All of us," Kitty said.

Rick looked up to the top of the building. "Something's going on," he said. "Hard to tell what, other than it's not friendly."

"How will we know if it worked?"

"If you see the Sentinels start milling around like they don't know what to do, that'll be a sign," Rick said. "If the transmitter up there is destroyed, they won't be able to hear each other."

Reinforcements for the Sentinels inside the Baxter Building were already arriving. From the north, three landed on the roof and disappeared.

Three others marched into view on Madison Avenue, taking up a guard position at 43rd Street.

Six Sentinels coming from the west landed on 42nd Street, between Madison and Fifth. Three of them split off and marched toward the intersection of Madison. Too close for comfort, Kitty thought—but as long as the mutants' powers weren't interacting with the environment, the Sentinels didn't seem to notice them. Either that, or the Sentinels were entirely focused on the armed attack on the Baxter Building.

Maybe it didn't matter. All that mattered was that Rachel was keeping herself alive, and the Sentinels were leaving them alone. For the moment, at least.

Apparently, Rick felt the same way. "Weapons down, FCA. Slow and discreet. Somewhere out of sight. We are out of here," he said. "No way we can take on the Sentinels. You coming?"

"No," Kitty said. "I'm not leaving my friends."

"You sure? I don't think things are going too well."

"All the more reason to stay," Kitty said.

"Well, good luck to you, then," Rick said. "FCA, disappear. Rendezvous at location Chuck."

The rest of the FCA soldiers melted away to the east, away from the visible Sentinels. They'd left their guns behind the canopy over the stairs down to the subway. Kitty felt a moment of alarm. What if the Sentinels noticed the guns? Under the circumstances, she guessed that would be enough for her and Rachel to be vaporized, no questions asked. They couldn't stay here, but she wasn't sure Rachel could be moved.

Rick lingered a moment longer. "Last chance. I'll take you both with me if you want to go." He looked at the Sentinels and back to Kitty. "If you're coming, now's the time."

"Not while they're still inside," Kitty said.

"All right, then," Rick said, and then he was gone.

The Sentinels stood their ground. One of them looked at Kitty and Rachel, then back at the Baxter Building. Their orders apparently did not include clearing the area of human flotsam lying against the railing at the head of the subway stairs.

It made sense. If the Sentinels could contain Logan, Storm, and Peter inside the building, what happened outside wouldn't matter. Kitty couldn't make a difference. Neither could Rachel. Magneto could cause some damage, but he was probably dead by now. Even if he wasn't, he might not be able to get himself out of the camp.

"Oh, no," Rachel said. Her eyes were closed, and her breathing was getting slower and shallower.

Kitty didn't dare ask.

PETER heard a sound like the release of an air brake—a quick, percussive blast of air. He pictured a hose bursting. Probably something had been weakened by the various acts of destruction performed in this room, and now it had let loose.

Ororo hadn't answered his question. "Ororo, we—"

Peter turned to her and stopped. Storm was

falling, pierced through the body by a six-foot steel spear. Behind her stood the Sentinel with the shattered face, arm extended, the firing tube visible at the base of its palm. Past that were more Sentinels, crowding into the control room.

The Sentinel tried to say something, but its vocal apparatus was too severely damaged. All that came out was another series of buzzing squawks and squeals—yet somehow to Peter they seemed arrogant and smug, as the first Omega-class Sentinel had been before Storm silenced it.

She fell to her hands and knees as Peter cried out, "Ororo!"

The Sentinel fired another spear, locking in on Peter's voice. It hit him square in the belly, but did no more than rock him back onto his heels. He counted three, four, five more over its shoulder forcing their way into the room.

Ororo tried to get up, but her legs weren't responding. She turned her head and locked eyes with Peter. He didn't need telepathy to know what she was thinking. It was there on her face, the same expression Rachel had worn when he'd set her down in the subway tunnel. Ororo knew she was going to die.

Her gaze bored into Peter, and already he mourned her loss—the leadership they had come to take for granted ever since Cyclops' departure, so many years ago. But she was not afraid. She was angry. Her anger blazed out in the form of static charges, short-circuiting equipment throughout the control room. Electricity flared from console panels, and Storm's hair stood on end. She grasped the shaft protruding from below her sternum, teeth bared. Then the electricity flickered out. Peter saw the light fade in her eyes, as well.

Peter roared, a pure animal sound that rejected everything he had ever stood for. Peace had died. Faith had died. Franklin, Logan, Ororo. Soon, Rachel...

And what of Kate? Alone in the street below, or fighting a doomed battle in the past, forever unreachable. She, too, was gone—or soon would be. Peter was the last. The last X-Man, the last mutant, the last soldier in a lost cause—fighting a future that existed only to destroy him and those he loved.

So be it, he thought.

He had known anger before, but now he knew hate.

CHAPTER 15

WHILE the X-Men were still picking themselves up off the ground—and Angel was still reorienting himself from the violent tumble through Storm's pocket hurricane—a second blast sounded from inside the Senate building. No wall collapsed this time. The sound was not an explosion, but a punch of such force it registered on the Richter scale.

Colossus shot out of the building in a high arc. Before Storm could slow him down or Angel could try to catch him, he landed flat on his back. The impact sent up a small explosion of turf, dirt, and shattered concrete from the plaza between the Senate building and the grassy part of the Mall.

A moment later, the Blob leaped through the same opening. "I told ya, Russkie!" he shouted.

"Nothin' can move me 'less I wanna be moved! But I can move myself no matter how heavy I am! And you're about to find out just how heavy—*whoof!*"

A crackling boom sounded from the military position a hundred yards away, and Blob's boast was cut off by the force of a concussion beam. Storm recognized the sound and, belatedly, the mobile artillery piece that had produced it. It was part of a Stark Industries advanced project, based on Tony Stark's repulsor technology. Stark must have licensed it to the military some time ago, before he'd gotten out of the defense-contracting business.

Blob's immense mass absorbed most of the beam's impact in mid-air. But when he was not in contact with the ground, even he was not immovable. The beam deflected him ever so slightly—just enough that when he came thundering back to earth, his feet punched a hole through the concrete of the plaza instead of Colossus' chest. Scrambling to his feet,

Colossus immediately charged to exploit the Blob's momentary disadvantage—but a second concussion beam hit him squarely in the back, blasting him across the plaza. He skidded to a halt in a plowed-up hill of shattered concrete, stunned by the impact.

"No!" Storm cried out. "We are your allies!"

Even as she said it, she knew the effort was futile. The Army forces would not take the trouble to distinguish one group of mutants from another, no matter what proclamations they might have seen from the Senate chamber. The Brotherhood had won that battle and successfully turned all mutants into perceived enemies. What remained, then, was to save Senator Kelly, subdue the Brotherhood, and escape to begin the counteroffensive against Kelly's pernicious bigotry.

The third concussion cannon fired, its blast crushing Avalanche against the Senate building's destroyed front wall. He disappeared in the falling rubble.

Storm heard cheers from the soldiers. She

wanted to cheer, too. The more of a pounding the Army inflicted on the Brotherhood, the more likely the X-Men were to accomplish their goal.

Blob charged after the recovering Colossus and pried up a huge slab of concrete, using it as a lever to tip Peter over backward and then crush him beneath it. Even in his organic-steel form, Peter was taking a terrible beating. He was going to need help.

No more salvos followed from the concussion cannons. Perhaps they needed time to recharge. That gives us an opening, Storm thought. But then a line of soldiers stepped forward with flamethrowers and began to lay down a wall of fire. Storm started to warn them away, but decided to save her breath. They wouldn't listen.

"Bad idea, gentlemen," Pyro said, almost crooning as he stepped forward. With a gesture, he brought the flames under his control. "Using fire against me? I do hope your armed services provide you with adequate pensions. Your survivors will need them."

The soldiers cut off their flamethrowers, but it was far too late. Pyro took the fire and shaped it into an immense demonic creature, reveling in the terror he caused. He could just as easily have deployed a simple wall of fire, but giving his creations a face and an impression of sentience made them so much more menacing. The creature loomed over the soldiers, who stumbled back, fleeing before it—but there was no way they could outrun it. Scorched footprints the size of a small car, spaced twenty feet apart, measured its progress across the plaza.

Angel swooped down in front of the flame creature. The creature turned its attention to him, giving the soldiers a few precious seconds to get away. Pyro muttered a string of profanities, struggling to maintain his creation's cohesiveness. The flame creature flailed and batted at Angel, who hovered and dipped just out of its reach. "Can't do this forever, gang!" he shouted. "Someone give a guy a hand and take Pyro out!"

After pounding on Colossus, Blob had

turned to Wolverine—but this time, he'd bitten off a little more than even he could chew. Wolverine didn't care how heavy an opponent was. Adamantium claws were not affected by mass.

"Whatsa matter, bub?" Logan taunted. "Thought you were invulnerable. You're not scared of these little ol' claws, are ya?"

Blob didn't answer. He was too busy heaving his bulk out of the way of Logan's claws. He ripped up slabs of concrete and held them up to protect himself, but Logan tore through them as fast as Blob could pick them up. Blob didn't dare get close enough to Logan to take a shot at him. He knew Logan would claw his immovable mass apart before he could even throw a punch.

Neither Blob nor Storm wanted that to happen, for different reasons. "Logan, stop!" she shouted, but Wolverine wasn't listening. The X-Men could not be seen killing people here. Logan, in his red fury, wasn't thinking of that. Storm was.

Help arrived from an unexpected source:

Pyro, who had regained control over his fire creation. With a two-handed motion, as if he were pulling taffy, he divided it in half. "Presto!" he proclaimed. "Parthenoflamesis! From one fire monster, I give you two!"

The two halves of the first monster grew in stature until both were larger than the original. Waves of heat shimmered off them, buckling the plaza below their feet. One of them continued to pursue Angel, but his powerful wings beat at it and blew parts of it away. He was using its own nature against it: Air was vital to fire, but too much air was lethal.

The other fire monster was a greater problem. It flowed suddenly across the expanse of the plaza and rose up to seize Logan in one incandescent claw. Logan cried out in uncharacteristic agony. He could handle a lot of pain, and he healed faster than just about any person on the planet, but even he could not survive being burned alive for long.

Angel's windy sparring with the other fire

monster gave Storm an idea. "Hold on, Logan!" she shouted. Storm flew straight up, gaining hundreds of feet of altitude in seconds before jackknifing down to dive straight toward Logan. The fire monster was drawing him in for what surely would be a fatal embrace.

"Haw haw, lookit that!" Blob said. "Not so tough now, are you...*bub*?"

Logan roared and sliced uselessly at the flame creature's arms, in the grip of an adversary even his claws could not harm.

But wind could. Storm had spent years investigating every potential use of her mutant powers; she knew that while lightning and hurricanes were the best blunt instruments at her disposal, more subtle methods of manipulating the elements also were available to her. Storm gathered the wind about her as she arrowed down, accelerating to more than two hundred miles per hour. When she slammed to a halt ten feet above the ground, she carried with her a bolus of wind that hit the fire monster with the power of a tornado concentrated into a single blow. It disintegrated into wisps.

Logan fell to the ground, his arms and torso visibly charred. The burns were bad enough that a normal man would have fallen instantly into fatal shock. But Logan stayed on his hands and knees, gritting his teeth as his flesh began to heal itself.

"We're right back where we started, Storm!" Pyro called out, goading her. "But I fear your animalistic friend is a bit worse for wear!"

Pyro returned his full attention to the surviving fire monster, using it as a vanguard to get closer to the endangered soldiers. Angel darted in behind him and landed a two-footed kick to his back, but retreated quickly as the fire monster nearly burned his wings off. Spiraling back up out of range, Angel saw the monster continue toward the soldiers' line. They fired at it with everything they had, but apparently Stark Industries had not supplied them with advanced anti-fire-monster weaponry.

Nightcrawler, having finally arrived in the

chamber, *bamf*ed over to Logan's side. "Logan, *mein verruckt freund,* are you all right?"

"I'll live," Logan growled. "But a few more seconds...I owe Storm, that's for sure. Man, 'Crawler, this *hurts*."

"For you to admit that, it must—what the *devil?!*"

Nightcrawler looked up, shocked. Logan followed his gaze and saw another Nightcrawler leaping toward them. "Wolverine, beware! That's not me!" this second Nightcrawler warned. "One of the Brotherhood must be a shapechanger!"

The two Nightcrawlers collided and grappled across the ground. Still reeling from his burns, Logan looked from one to the other, mystified.

"Whoever you are, villain," one of them said, "you've bitten off more than you can chew. I've spent a long time growing comfortable in this skin, and I like being unique. I don't take kindly to doppelgangers."

"Neither do I!" said the other.

Under normal circumstances, Logan would have been able to tell the two Nightcrawlers apart. It was mighty tough to fool his sense of smell. But his nose was still recovering from inhaling fire, and the two figures looked identical. So he opted for a more direct and decisive approach. A shapechanger might be able to look like Nightcrawler, but it sure wouldn't be able to teleport like him. Logan unsheathed his claws.

Storm flew over, alarmed. "Logan, what are you doing?"

"Figuring out which one of these twins is the real Nightcrawler," Logan said. "He oughta be able to teleport away when he sees these coming."

"Sheathe your claws," she said.

"We're in a fight here, 'Ro," Logan said. "It's not debate time."

Ororo stepped in front of him. "Logan, either sheathe your claws or use them on me first."

Wolverine lowered his head and leaned into her, keeping his claws back but poised. "That can be arranged, babe."

The two Nightcrawlers were still pounding each other. Angel was taking drastic measures against Pyro's fire monster, pulling individual soldiers up and over the barricades to safety—despite one of them taking a shot at him. Blob was tearing up chunks of the plaza and throwing them at the soldiers—or maybe at Colossus; it was hard to tell. Smoke from small fires in the Senate building and on the Mall obscured the battlefield.

None of that mattered. Wolverine needed to settle a thing or two with Ororo.

"I am the leader of the X-Men," she said, keeping her tone level and holding her position. Wolverine's claws were inches from gutting her. "You will use your claws when I tell you to use your claws. No other time."

"I wouldn't take that from Cyclops," Wolverine growled.

"What matters is not what you and Cyclops would do, but what you and I will do," Ororo answered. "If you go slashing away at every problem, what will the image of mutants be?"

"They're gonna hate us either way," Logan said. "I'm not in this for the gratitude."

"Then—if you do not care about the humans—care about your fellow mutants who will suffer if you turn public opinion against them. You are strong. You are fast. You are nearly invulnerable. Use your claws only against the deadliest and most powerful foes."

Wolverine held her gaze a moment longer, then retracted his claws with a snap. "Okay, Storm," he said—using her X-moniker, she thought, to let her know just how angry he was. "We'll do it your way for now. But this conversation ain't finished. Not by a long shot."

Then the ground bucked and heaved under them, throwing Logan off balance and flinging Storm into the air. Avalanche, looking at the undulating strip of concrete and earth he'd raised, quipped, "Lady, since you and your hairy pal would obviously rather feud than fight, it seems only fair I should give you a ride to somewhere you can do it in peace!"

"Logan, grab my hand!" Storm reached down and barely missed Logan's grasp. He fell, sprawling, on the face of Avalanche's debris wave.

"Too late! If you hadn't gone and got squeamish, we wouldn't have this problem!" Logan shouted back. "Now who's gonna help Nightcrawler?"

"I want no help, Wolverine!" one of the Nightcrawlers said.

The other seemed to agree. "I intend to finish this fight on my own!"

The force of the seismic ripple carried Logan away from the Nightcrawlers and brought him to a rolling halt in a rain of concrete chunks. A flying metal trash can struck him in the back of the head. He looked up and saw Colossus running toward him, carrying a thirty-foot section of I-beam in a pole-vault position. "Wolverine, come with me! I need your assistance to handle the Blob!"

"I'll handle him, all right," Logan said, showing his claws again.

"No! I have a better plan. It takes him out and leaves him alive."

"You call that better?" Logan sighed. "Okay, Petey, ya peacenik. What do you want to do?"

The Blob threw another huge concrete chunk, like a discus. It hit one of the concussion cannons and smashed it over backward, breaking off its barrel and scattering its crew. The other two cannons had just about powered up again, if the crackling along their barrels was any indication. Blob tore up another discus and snarled, "Think ya can zap me? Try this, instead!"

Clouds began to roll in, too fast to be natural, and Logan saw a dust storm kicking up across the Mall. Then Avalanche came running out of the storm, raging against Ororo and heaving the earth randomly around him in pure incoherent fury.

Near the military position, Angel was still lifting endangered soldiers away from Pyro's fire monster. The soldiers' remaining heavy equipment had begun to burn and melt from its approach. Pyro followed, playing tricks with the secondary fires his monster created—and playing cat-and-mouse with Angel. The airborne mutant flapped his wings furiously, creating powerful downdrafts to extinguish the flames as fast as Pyro could fan them.

"I knew I shoulda skewered that limey when I had the chance," Wolverine said. "No matter what 'Roro said."

"You will not be surprised to learn that I disagree," Colossus said. He nodded at a point on the ground. "Quickly. Kneel."

Wolverine did, and Colossus laid the I-beam across Logan's right shoulder. "I get you, pal," Wolverine replied. "Like Archimedes said: Gimme a big enough lever, and I can move the world."

The Blob cocked his arm to throw again, and Colossus heaved down on the end of the I-beam. "Blob!" Avalanche shouted. The Blob started to react, but it was too late. With Wolverine as its fulcrum, the beam tilted—its other end rising up to catch Blob like a see-saw just as he was releasing his next missile. The I-beam lifted him up, the principles of vector physics imparting tremendous angular momentum to his mass, and flung him high into the air.

"*Yeeeooowwww!*" he screamed, amazed that he'd been lifted off his feet. Wolverine had felt his Adamantium bones grind together from the force the beam had pressed onto his back. Even when he wasn't making himself immovable, Fred J. Dukes was one massive piece of work.

"Now comes part two," Colossus said, eyeing Blob's arc through the air.

"I'm curious," Wolverine said. "Did we move him, or move the earth out from under him? I'm gonna need a chiropractor."

"I am not sure any chiropractors work on Adamantium, my friend," Colossus said.

Avalanche was about to create another seismic event. Storm, in the air above him, began to gather wind and rain—but she had already depleted the immediate area to create her spray inside the Senate building. Late October in

Washington, D.C., was not a humid time, but as Storm concentrated moisture and energy, clouds began to roll in from over the Potomac. A bolt of lightning wouldn't fry Avalanche, she knew, but it would make him uncomfortable enough that he could not muster another serious attack.

She struck him with sleet and snow, coming down out of the seventy-degree sky. She kicked up dust devils around him to interfere with his vision. He struck out furiously in all directions, sending shock waves across the Mall. If they'd been inside a building, it would have shaken itself to gravel.

THE TREMOR bounced the brawling Nightcrawlers up into the air, separating them. When they returned to Earth, they faced each other again.

"You are not me," Kurt said. "So who are you?"

His double sparred, feinted, spun, and kicked just as he did—as if the other had lived in Kurt's body all his life. Who was this? Kurt struck fast and hard, disdaining his teleportation out of a sense of mingled anger and fair play. On the one hand, he wanted to kill this impostor. On the other hand, something about the situation piqued his vexing tendency to test himself both physically and emotionally. Could he meet this doppelganger and fight him—without using abilities the doppelganger could not have?

Could he, in other words, defeat himself?

The other reason he shied away from teleportation, of course, was more practical. If he were to beat the doppelganger into unconsciousness quickly, the double might not revert to his original shape. Then the investigation would be delayed—and time was something the X-Men did not have. This was clearly a Brotherhood member, and Nightcrawler needed to identify which one as quickly as possible.

So he would fight his double, and taunt his double, and in the end wear his double down and force him to reveal his true nature.

"You are not me, either," the double said.

"*Stimmt,*" Kurt replied, and they came at each other again.

WHEN she saw the Blob catapulted into the air, Storm paused in surprise. How had—? Then she looked down and saw Wolverine standing up, shrugging off the long steel beam. Storm almost cracked a smile. Her concentration wavered for a moment.

Then she saw Avalanche, refocused on Colossus and Wolverine. Storm's smile faded. She was going to have to hit him now—with everything she had. But she would not kill.

Then she figured out the second part of Peter's plan, and her smile came back.

The Blob was in the air for more than seven seconds, but less than eight. That, as it turned out, was exactly how much time Colossus needed to twist the I-beam until it snapped, discard half of it, and cock the other half over his right shoulder as if he had grown up in Brooklyn instead of Siberia.

Blob fell back within range, tumbling through the air. He saw Colossus. He saw the broken-off I-beam. His eyes widened. Colossus swung.

The impact bent the I-beam into a comma with a sound loud enough to hurt Wolverine's ears. Blob rocketed over the plaza—straight toward Avalanche, whose eyes were visibly widening through the slot in his helmet. "Blob! No!" he yelled.

The sound of Blob's hurtling mass hitting Avalanche was almost as loud as the crack of Colossus' makeshift bat. Avalanche was leveled and out cold, his helmet knocked off and spinning across the plaza. The impact barely slowed Blob's progress. He continued on another hundred feet or so before tumbling over the broken plaza and coming to rest not far from the military cordon.

"That is what you'd call a frozen rope," Wolverine said.

"I am unfamiliar with that expression," Colossus said. "Also, I thought you were Canadian."

"I've spent a lot of time south of the border," Logan said. "Hard to be here this long and not catch a ballgame once in a while."

"It is a long trip to the Bronx," Colossus said.

"For a good game, it's worth it. Plus, there's always the Mets. And what, you never heard of the Blue Jays?"

Colossus didn't answer.

That was two of the Brotherhood down. "Logan! Peter! Are you all right?" Storm descended toward them.

"We're fine, 'Ro," Wolverine said. "Let's handle Pyro. I'm not done bustin' heads yet."

"I'm afraid it's my turn, boys," Storm said. "I didn't bring all these clouds in for nothing."

She accelerated away from them, up into the sky again. Pyro was guiding his fire monster toward the soldiers. Two of the concussion cannons were slag, and the third lay in pieces from Blob's concrete barrage. The soldiers were trying to keep the fire monster—and Pyro—

away from the civilians behind the cordon, who lacked the common sense to stay a prudent distance away from explosions and fire.

Storm had a solution to all those problems, however. Below her, Wolverine and Colossus were running toward the fighting Nightcrawlers, swinging wide around the inert bodies of Blob and Avalanche.

Storm got to altitude and spread her arms. Static electricity from the gathered clouds flickered, intensified, and licked down toward her in the form of lightning. Crackling along her skin, the lightning spread her cloak wide.

"Hell of a show she puts on," Logan said. "Her only problem is she doesn't know who needs killing."

"Let it go," Colossus said. He knew what Logan was getting at. "Imagine you strike at Kurt with your claws, thinking he will disappear. What if you are wrong, and he doesn't?"

It was tough to shrug and run at the same time, but Logan managed. "I trust him. You'll see."

They were close to the Nightcrawlers, who were very evenly matched. This was to be expected, certainly, but Kurt's natural use of his abilities should have given him the advantage. One way or another, Logan thought, they were going to get this figured out. The backs of his hands itched, like they always did when he wanted to bare his claws.

When they were less than fifty yards from the Nightcrawlers, with the fire monster pinning the soldiers against the cordon and Pyro following close behind, Logan felt something in the air change. He looked up and saw Ororo lean her head back, her mouth opening in a smile of pure ecstasy. Electricity flared around her. With a peal of thunder, she brought the rain.

Ororo had read once that the average storm cloud weighed approximately five thousand tons. She had just brought several of them together, and now she made the smallest adjustment to the clouds' chemistry and temperature. What had been suspended water vapor became billions of droplets of rain, falling in sheets that emptied the clouds in seconds. Rain crashed down over Pyro and his fiery creation, snuffing it out with so much water that even the steam of its vanishing was swept away before anyone could see it.

Pyro didn't last much longer. He looked up and saw what Storm was doing. He tried to use the lightning as seeds for new fiery creations, but Storm snuffed them out as quickly as they were born. Then the rain hit him with the power of a firehose.

Wolverine saw Pyro go down, flattened into the concrete of the plaza by the force of the downpour. Serves him right, Logan thought. Even if I didn't get to cut him up. Ah well, everyone's gotta make sacrifices.

He looked over at the soldiers. Already they were forming up, preparing to come after the X-Men. Figures, Logan thought. Every time it has a chance to be over, it's not over. Maybe it'll be this way no matter what Kate does in Kitty's body.

Maybe we're all headed for the Sentinels, anyway. But even if that was true, he was going to fight it every step of the way.

KURT was getting tired. But so was his doppelganger. They had parried and struck, attacked and countered, battered each other with fist and foot until both were panting and growing sloppy.

Kurt decided to try a favorite feint of his, involving a dropped shoulder that led to a reverse spin taking advantage of the opponent's hesitation upon seeing the initial feint. If the opponent was slightly tired, but still trying to react as if he was fully capable, the timing would work.

Kurt dipped a shoulder as if he were tensing to lead with a kick from the opposite leg. Then, flexing that leg, Kurt spun into a reverse kick. He aimed high enough that the doppelganger would have trouble bringing up his tired arms to block the kick, but low enough that he wouldn't be able to contract his fatigued core muscles fast enough to duck.

It was harder than Kurt had anticipated to not use his teleportation abilities—but also more satisfying. He felt his heel make solid contact with bone and followed through, the momentum of his leg carrying his body around on the axis of his other leg to face the toppling doppelganger...

...who began to transform as he hit the ground. "*Unglaublich!*" Kurt said.

Not he. She.

So much for all my assumptions, thought Kurt. "You're... Mystique!"

ANGEL, sweeping down from the sky after seeing Storm's watery coup de grace on Pyro, hesitated over the fighting Nightcrawlers and watched as one of them delivered a decisive shot to the other. Angel drifted lower, unsure whether to help the downed Nightcrawler or congratulate the one that was still standing. Then he saw one of the Nightcrawlers begin to change, although the blended form continued to have indigo skin, pupilless yellow eyes…

My God, Angel thought.

"You?" Kurt said, staring at Mystique. "You're the shapechanger?"

Mystique smiled at Nightcrawler. Angel thought it was the saddest and most hateful expression he had ever seen.

"Your skin," Kurt continued. "Your eyes. If this is your true form, *mein Gott*. We are so alike!"

The soldiers who were not already engaged in binding Blob and Avalanche flooded across the plaza toward them. They didn't have much time to wrap this up. The soldiers would be on them in moments.

"Could it be, Kurt Wagner," Mystique said, emphasizing the hard W and short A of the German pronunciation, "that you are not as unique as you once thought?"

Shocked, Nightcrawler moved toward her. "Who are you?"

Then the soldiers were surrounding them, screaming for Nightcrawler to put his hands in the air and get on the ground. Mystique stepped back easily, melting into them, her features and clothes already shifting again.

"Who are you?" Kurt screamed. He looked from soldier to soldier for some trace of the woman who bore so many features common to his own. But there was no way to pick her out, now. He began teleporting in quick hops through the entire contracting ring of soldiers. They pointed guns at him, screaming threats and commands while their fellow soldiers dove out of the fields of fire.

"Vamoose, buddy!" Angel warned him, swooping down and spreading his wings to slow the soldiers' approach. They shouted orders, aiming their rifles upward and warning him to stay where he was—but they didn't come any closer.

Kurt and Angel stood together. Wolverine joined them. He was healing now, but the effects of Pyro's monster were still plain on his skin.

Madness, Kurt thought. *Unglaublich!*

"The Army's got Blob, Pyro, and Avalanche,"

Angel said. "Now they're looking to add the X-Men to their collection. That was Mystique, right? Where'd she go?"

Storm angled in as Nightcrawler said, "*Keine Ahnung*. She blended in, changed her shape again. Who is she really? She looks so much like me. Or perhaps it is the other way around."

"It appears that all our actions have not changed the Army's mind about us," Storm said. "But I have a solution. These clouds might prove useful again." She brought the clouds down to drown the Mall in a thick ground fog. "We'll rendezvous at the airport once we find Kitty."

"Kate," Peter said.

"Yes, Kate."

"And Charlie," Wolverine said. "Has he been in touch with anybody? I haven't heard a peep."

None of them had. They ran through the fog, trying to stay unobtrusive as the Army patrols swept the Mall for anything having to do with the mutant incursion and its aftermath. Flashlight beams pierced the fog. Officers called out instructions to form perimeters and search grids.

"Quickly," Storm whispered. "We must seek out Professor Xavier. Given all that has happened, he would certainly have contacted us if he were able."

They headed toward the Senate building, stopping at the corner farthest from the Capitol. None of them could see far in the fog, but the traces of the battle were everywhere—from the pieces of concrete torn from the plaza to the gaping holes in the Senate office building.

Kate Pryde was in there somewhere. Doubtless she had separated from the team to protect Senator Kelly. What was she doing now? Where was Destiny, the only member of the Brotherhood they had not seen since the initial confrontation in the hearing chamber?

Mystique was on the run. Three other members of the Brotherhood were in the Army's custody. Now the X-Men had to make sure that Kate Pryde's horrific future did not come to pass for them all.

CHAPTER 16

RACHEL was fading. Kitty knew it, but she could do nothing about it. She couldn't do anything about anything. All she could do was watch. Tomorrow, a nuclear strike would destroy New York and countless other cities. If she was still alive then, she would die. The story of mutant-kind would end.

A boom sounded from high up, within the Baxter Building. A Sentinel burst through the wall, falling in a shower of glass and steel, limp and tumbling. It landed in the middle of the street with a deafening crash, followed by the smaller pings and clangs of the debris falling around it.

Other Sentinels ran to it, broadcasting alerts and status reports. "Sentinel Omega-J7," one of them said. "Do you still function?"

Sentinel Omega-J7 did not answer.

Another thunderous crash from above heralded another falling Sentinel. This one landed on the trunk of an abandoned car, flipping the vehicle up into the air end over end. The car slammed into another Sentinel, staggering it.

Kitty looked up at the Baxter Building as Sentinel reinforcements lifted off from the street, rocketing up to the level of their command center. Six of them reached the gaping hole at once. Something struck one of them squarely in the face, smashing away part of its head. Its boot rockets cut out; it dropped straight down four hundred feet, punching through the sidewalk and embedding itself waist-deep in the ground. Sparks and flares shot out of the hole it had made, and it began to burn.

The other five powered up their torso repulsors. Another missile from inside the building hit one of those repulsor lenses, overloading the mechanism. The Sentinel exploded like a bomb, pieces of it ricocheting off the other four and shattering more windows. Its arms left curving trails of smoke as they fell, landing after its lower torso and legs—a long time before its head, which bounced south across the intersection past Kitty and Rachel. It came to rest on the sidewalk in front of the New York Public Library.

The remaining four Sentinels reset their formation and fired their repulsors simultaneously. Kitty saw detonations inside the building. She couldn't believe anyone could have survived— but someone had. A long metal beam, thrown like a spear, impaled one of the Sentinels as it tried to enter the hole. It squealed, the sound picked up and amplified by several other Sentinels down on the street as they relayed an emergency alert. Then its grip on the edge of the hole slipped, and it fell, bouncing against the side of the Baxter Building twice on its way down before landing almost directly on top of its partially decapitated comrade.

Madison Avenue was littered with pieces of Sentinels, and Kitty felt a predator's glee at the sight. All of you die, she thought. All of you, for all the people you've killed.

Peter—for surely it was Peter up there, as neither Ororo nor Logan could have thrown those missiles with such force—was not done yet. Now she saw him, at the edge of the floor, reaching out for the closest Sentinel and dragging it headfirst into the building. He seemed enraged, almost possessed, stronger than ever before. The Sentinel's legs kicked, then went limp and hung over the edge.

More reinforcements landed on the Baxter Building's roof. Others entered on the ground floor, using an entrance refitted for their size. Still more lifted off to force their way into the command center directly.

Kitty's fierce glee evaporated suddenly as she realized she had not seen Ororo or Logan fighting. "Oh, no," she said.

"Yeah," Rachel said.

Kitty looked down at her. "You knew?"

"Every time," Rachel said with her eyes

closed. "I feel them. I felt Franklin." She started to cry, tears cutting pale tracks through the grime on her face. They were both filthy from their time in the tunnels and from the dust kicked up by the battles. "I felt Logan. I felt Ororo. I felt every one of the FCA."

Kitty tried to clean the tears from Rachel's face, but all she did was smear the grime around. "Magneto?" she asked. "Him, too?"

"I don't know," Rachel said. "I wasn't thinking about him, he was farther away…" Her energy failed her, and she fell silent.

Kitty looked up again. A series of flashes from within the building strobed out into the sky, dislodging more rubble. It cascaded down onto Madison Avenue, crushing two of the responding Sentinels and obscuring the building's lower floors behind another rolling billow of dust.

"Peter," Rachel said softly.

"What about him?" Kitty asked.

"He's dead," Rachel said. "They're all dead."

Fires raged in the Baxter Building's upper floors, but Sentinels were approaching from all directions. More and more of them arrived from other parts of the city, some marching on the street and others flying in tight V-formations from across the Hudson River. Their motions appeared well-coordinated.

Rick had told Kitty that as long as the Sentinels were communicating, the control antennas were still working.

The X-Men had failed.

"Kitty, it's time," Rachel said. "Time for you to go home."

Kitty caught her breath. Home, she thought. Yes. Get out of this terrible place. But then she looked again at Rachel, her face drawn with pain and the effort of keeping herself alive.

"I don't have much time left," Rachel said.

"What if I stayed? What if this is what was supposed to happen?"

"No. We might…you going back isn't going to change this future. Maybe nothing can be unmade, once it exists. But you might create a split in the future, and you'll get to live in the better one. That's what I would hope for. You should…" Rachel had to stop and breathe for a moment. "You should hope so, too," she finished.

"It's destiny, though, right? I was meant to come here. It couldn't just be so I could watch everyone die."

"You're going back," Rachel said. "Then the Sentinels are going to come and kill me. That's just what's going to happen, kid. No way around it now."

Her other self, her older self, wouldn't know that was about to happen. If the mind swap were reversed now, Kate Pryde would arrive back in her native time staring down the barrel of a dozen Sentinels' guns. Or a hundred. How long would she survive? Would she die knowing all of her friends—and Peter—had died before her?

Or would she just die?

"I'll try, Kitty. I'll try…" Rachel trailed off. Kitty couldn't tell whether she was alive or dead.

The Sentinels loomed closer. Some of them turned to look at Kitty and Rachel, then looked away again, still focused on damage control at their command center. Lower-ranking Sentinels arrived and started cleaning up the debris, scattered along the entire block from 42nd to 43rd streets.

Kitty sat still, cradling Rachel and feeling each shallow rise and fall of the older mutant's breath.

"I should have done something," Kitty said.

"You did," Rachel breathed. "You were here. You got us this far."

"I did nothing. I watched all my friends die."

"Me, too," Rachel said, her voice only audible because Kitty bent close to hear her.

We lost, Kitty thought. I'm never going to grow up. I'm going to die in this future. And Kate—*me*, this me I started to imagine because everyone talked about her—she failed, too.

"What do I do now?" Kitty asked. "Do I have to do anything to help you?"

Rachel didn't answer.

"Rachel?" Kitty said. She leaned down again and listened. "Rachel?"

I'm the only one, Kitty thought. The last living mutant, but for how long? Everything around her blurred; she squeezed her eyes shut to clear her vision of tears. Crying was pointless now. If she was the last mutant, and if she was going to be stranded here in this future, she was going to have to get herself together and figure out how to survive.

Until the bombs started falling, anyway.

She wanted to give up. She couldn't help it. If she was going to die anyway, why not go out in some blaze of pointless glory? She could take a Sentinel with her, maybe more than one. That was one thing she'd learned here, at least.

Kitty eased herself out from under Rachel and set her head down gently on the sidewalk. Kitty's coat was soaked through with Rachel's blood. She stood up and looked again at the top floors of the Baxter Building. Sentinels were moving in and out, already beginning the repairs and reconstruction. They didn't know they only had another day to exist. Would they care? Probably not. They had a directive, and that directive was all that mattered to them.

A thought occurred to her. If she sacrificed herself, would the nuclear strike be averted? The Sentinels would have no mission objectives remaining in North America. Would they immediately move on Europe, bringing the battlefield with them? How many lives might that save? There were too many variables for her to predict, too many uncertainties.

The only thing Kitty knew for sure was that she was never going home. That knowledge, and her utter isolation, paralyzed her for a moment. She stood watching the Sentinels with the strange premonition that she was observing the successors to the human race. No nuclear strike could destroy them all. Somewhere, a Sentinel factory would survive. More of them would be built, and more and more, until the Earth belonged to them alone. And then what would they do?

The question would matter only to them.

Something was moving in the sky to the north. It was only two or three blocks away, too small to be a Sentinel, and it lacked the telltale flare of their boot rockets. It was man-shaped, though, moving slowly toward her at the level of the upper floors of the taller buildings along Madison Avenue. Something about it…

Kitty gasped. Her heart leaped.

"Magneto," she said.

She was not alone after all.

HE RODE lines of force, invisible to all but him. The ruined streets of Manhattan four hundred feet below looked like pockets and reservoirs, lines and fields of conductivity and resistance. They were part of him, extensions of him, the magnetic field of the Earth itself like a nervous system that extended his perceptions and powers. Ahead, the Baxter Building burned. Magneto could see the concentration of electromagnetic energies focused in the spires of its rooftop antenna nest.

The Sentinels' internal devices alerted them to the use of his mutant powers. He saw and felt all of them at once, in their dozens. They marched along the street, worked inside the destroyed areas of the Baxter Building, arrayed themselves on its roof, flew in tight groupings from all directions toward him.

He halted, letting the steel skeletons of the buildings on either side of him provide the balance of repulsion he required to stay aloft. His legs hung below him, useless but not needed, and he appeared to stand on air.

The Sentinels boomed out their warnings. "Mutant 067, your use of powers is prohibited. Cease or be terminated."

Interesting, he thought. Even now they do not strike first. They need mutants—at least a few.

And a few was all they had. Fewer even than an hour before, was his guess. He saw none of his fellow inmates from the camp. He did, however, see the traces of their presence in the heavy damage to the Baxter Building and in the crushed and dismembered Sentinels littering the street below. They had fought valiantly. In all likelihood, they had died.

A dozen Sentinels ringed him in the air, at a distance of less than fifty yards. One of them repeated its warning. "Mutant 067, your use of powers is—"

"Yes," he said. "I know."

The Sentinel paused to process this ambiguous statement. He allowed himself a moment to savor its confusion, then he thrust his arms out. A torus of magnetic repulsion expanded outward from him, moving at the speed of the Earth's rotation—nearly one thousand miles per hour. It hit the Sentinels all at once, and all their metallic components instantly repelled each other at the same speed. A dozen Sentinels became a debris field in the blink of an eye, briefly hanging in the air like a ring with Magneto as the planet holding it in orbit. Their internal fluids fell in a shower to the street below, along with the Sentinels' plastic and glass and rubber components. He held the ring for a moment, enjoying the sight and letting it stand as a statement to the rest of the Sentinels. This was his announcement: *Magneto is here*.

Then he let it go. The debris fell in a spreading rain, cascading down over several blocks of street and rooftop.

Missiles flew toward him from the Baxter Building's rooftop and from Sentinels flying in from the west. He turned them easily; each found a new target, blasting the flying formations out of the sky. "More!" Magneto cried out. "Are there not more of you?"

There were, rising toward him from the streets all around, their torso and palm repulsors glowing. Magneto grinned. He knew repulsor technology was based on the creation and channelling of muons—and muons were strongly affected by electromagnetism. "Yes," he said. He waited.

"Mutant 067," the nearest Sentinel said. "You will cease."

"I will not," Magneto said.

Their repulsors discharged all at once. Magneto created a sphere of magnetic energy around himself, redirecting the streams of muons and the heat created by their decay. The sphere flashed a blinding white, like a miniature sun in the artificial canyon of Madison Avenue. The energy was nearly too much for him to handle, but handle it he did.

Then he released it.

The combined energy of all the Sentinels' repulsor beams expanded away from him. The wave washed over the Sentinels and the facades of nearby buildings, burning everything it touched to slag and ashes. Past one hundred meters, the muons' decay reached the point where they no longer gave off heat. The tiny supernova winked out, leaving only fires burning in the buildings and on the street.

The Baxter Building was just ahead. This would be Magneto's piece de resistance. The satellites that were surely watching from Europe would see what he was about to do, and they would take note. What action that would prompt was uncertain. But even if he were the last surviving mutant in the western hemisphere, Magneto would send a message to the world that mutants were not finished just yet.

He drifted forward and saw, amid the wreckage on the street below the Baxter Building's east face, a small figure running. Looking closer, he smiled. Kate Rasputin. Another still lived.

That made his mission all the more important. All his life, Magneto had fought not for himself but for other mutants. Now, unexpectedly, he was given the chance to fight for other mutants again.

Sentinels on the street below were firing metal spears at him. He deflected them with barely a thought. Why had he allowed this to go on so long? Perhaps he had been weak. Perhaps his judgment had been clouded. Perhaps he had feared to act decisively, lest decisive action inadvertently harm those precious to him.

None of those things mattered now.

From the ruined upper floors of the Baxter Building, repulsor beams reached out toward him. He bent them aside. A row of Omega-class Sentinels stood in the opening. Within the building, he could sense the concentrated flow and swirl of electromagnetism around what must be a plasma core. A force field, constructed to resist the intrusion of matter and energy both. He felt it, probed it, and understood the patterns of the particles that composed it.

He could not destroy it. The Sentinels had constructed it wisely, using a plasma composed of particles unresponsive to magnetism. Everything inside that core was driven by the other binding forces that held matter together. It was pure information, and the Sentinels picked and chose tiny bits of it to compose into the broadcasts that gave them their orders and kept them synchronized across the North American continent.

Below, two of the Sentinels confronted Kate. Irritated by the distraction, Magneto tore them apart, strewing the pieces away from her. "Get out of here, Kate Rasputin," he called down. She shouted something back at him, but he did not hear what. He pointed, south and away. She ran.

The rush of adrenaline that had sustained Magneto started to abate. Again he was exhausted, and this time he would not be allowed the grace of time to recover. He began to descend, letting himself ride the opposing lines of the steel-framed buildings down to the street.

It galled him to give up the freedom of flight and return to his crippled and earthbound state, but he would need every particle of energy he could muster if his last gesture were not to be as futile as the brave deaths of the rest—for surely none of the rest had survived. That Kate had was a small miracle, if miracles there were. Magneto had never seen evidence of any, and had witnessed quite enough cruelty to argue they did not exist.

His feet touched the street, and he let himself down gently. He considered using the strips of metal threaded through his jumpsuit to keep himself upright, but any distraction of his powers from the main focus could prove fatal at this point. Fatigue buzzed in his head; he was having trouble focusing his vision. Sentinels tracked his trajectory and surrounded him on the street.

He wondered where Kate had gone, and hoped she had heeded his warning to put some distance between him and her. Proximity to Magneto was a poor survival strategy, and always had been. That was one more irony of his life's work.

"Mutant 067," one of the Sentinels said.

"My name is Magneto," he answered. "Are you afraid that when we are all dead you will have only an empty directive? What will you do then?"

"That is not your concern," the Sentinel said. "You will be taken for final analysis and terminated. As you should have been before."

"You can't win, you know," Magneto said, even though he did not believe it. "The rest of the world has seen what you do. They will band together and destroy you."

"Our directive must be fulfilled," the Sentinel

responded. "Now conversation will cease."

It bent down and picked up Magneto, settling him in the palm of its hand and closing its fingers over him—not to crush, but to contain him. He took advantage of every precious second to rest—closing his eyes, letting the architecture of the command center's data core wash again through his mind. Again he reached the same conclusion: He could not destroy it.

"Your exercise of your powers was futile," the Sentinel said.

"The ending of that book is not yet written," Magneto answered.

"Figurative language indicates evasion," the Sentinel said.

"Ah," Magneto said. "Allow me to explain in a language you will be sure to understand."

"Further use of your powers will result in immediate termination," the Sentinel said.

"Yes," Magneto said. "I understand."

KITTY had heard Magneto call her name, and

she had seen him warn her away. Running away to the south, she had stopped across from the library. She was torn between the primal urge to survive and another urge, only slightly less primal, to keep contact with the only other living member of her kind.

She had seen Magneto destroy Sentinel after Sentinel, seemingly without effort, and she rejoiced. Then she saw him sink slowly to the ground, and her spirits fell. Now he was in the grip of the enemy, literally, and she had an awful feeling she knew what would happen next. She was going to witness the death of the last mutant in North America other than her.

Her mind raced through different fantastic scenarios. She imagined herself on a ship, seeing the European coast come into view over the horizon. Boats would come to meet her and welcome her. They would tell her everything was all right. The European powers would save her, would oppose and destroy the Sentinels without pushing the red button. Maybe the technological savants of Wakanda would have an answer. Their shining silver craft would fill the skies over New York, rescuing her and saving millions from death by fire and fallout and famine.

Or maybe this was all a terrible dream, a prophetic warning about something happening back in her time. Soon she would awaken in her bed at Xavier's school. She would tell the rest of the X-Men about it over breakfast; they would tease her, but not cruelly. She would not be alone.

She was crying again, crouched in a bus shelter across from the library. The group of Sentinels moved toward the Baxter Building, keeping a tight circle around the one bearing Magneto. She could not see him.

A vibration rose in the air around her—almost a sound but not quite. It registered in her ears, but also in her bones and in the struts of the shelter around her. It intensified. She heard one of the Sentinels say something.

Then the group of Sentinels blew apart. Kitty flinched as a piece of Sentinel armor shattered the bus shelter's Plexiglas wall. She scrambled around the other side of it, finding a protected spot in the recessed doorway of a building. She looked back toward the Baxter Building. What had Magneto done?

He was there, hovering in the air with the severed hand of a Sentinel serving as a seat. He rose higher, arms spread and head thrown back, and Kitty felt the vibration increase again. An almost tectonic groan began to sound from somewhere nearby. Concrete dust showered down the facades of buildings up and down Madison Avenue, along with shards of brick and marble. The groan grew louder. In a moment of terror and exhilaration, Kitty understood.

A series of loud pops sounded from the Baxter Building—sporadically at first but then faster, until they sounded like firecrackers. The building's remaining intact windows shattered, falling in a glittering curtain, exposing the interior from ground to rooftop.

Magneto still hung in the air. She thought

she saw his mouth moving, but could not imagine what he might be saying. His chin fell to his chest, but his arms remained spread. She could see ripples like convection in the air around him.

Almost imperceptibly, the shape of the Baxter Building began to change. Its metal sides screamed, became concave. Its roofline tilted and sagged. Sentinels streamed through the sky from every direction, but something prevented them from getting too close.

Magneto dropped one arm, and an invisible force dragged abandoned cars and pieces of Sentinels into a circular pattern. The building itself twisted in that same direction, its girders shrieking and huge chunks of concrete cracking loose to crash down into the street.

First, the Sentinels fired everything they had at Magneto, but he took no notice of them. Their missiles tore holes in the surrounding buildings; their repulsor beams diffused and died. He dropped his other arm, and the Baxter Building crumpled inward.

A dust cloud rose on the street—roiling higher, almost obscuring Magneto. Through it Kitty could see the dull glow of fires flaring inside the building. An entire corner of the roof peeled off, carrying with it a spidery collection of girders and beams. Magneto lifted his head and then held still for a suspended moment. The vibrations around Kitty paused, and she realized she'd been holding her breath.

As she inhaled, so did Magneto, lifting his arms and bringing them together in a clap. It made no sound that Kitty could hear, but the Baxter Building collapsed into itself with a sound she would never forget. As it disappeared into the dust and smoke of its own disintegration, a titanic explosion destroyed the buildings on either side of it. Magneto vanished in the fireball that billowed out of the wreckage, washing over the buildings across Madison Avenue and mushrooming up into the sky.

Kitty stood, thunderstruck. In her numb daze, she noticed two things. The Sentinels hovering in the sky after the explosion were no longer moving in unison. It took her some time to realize the significance of this.

Second, she saw a light in the east. It was almost dawn. She had never expected to see another one. Incongruously, she realized this was the first time she had ever stayed up all night.

CHAPTER 17

DESTINY waited, knowing what would happen. As Mystique had guessed, Senator Kelly would return to his office. There, he would gather up what was most important to him—files, personal belongings, and so forth—before trying to make his escape. Whatever his feelings about mutants, Robert Kelly could not be called a coward. He believed what he believed, and acted on his beliefs. This position, to Destiny's mind, earned him the respect one felt for an enemy who tested one's abilities—before, of course, yielding or dying, because the sporting fair-play school of battle never favored the underdog.

Ever. And mutants were permanent underdogs.

Permanent, Destiny mused. An interesting word to use, for one who could see potential futures born and dying in every moment, every action, every hesitation and impulsive choice. Now she was seeing a door opening, a man entering. And even as those things happened—even as Senator Kelly stopped upon seeing Destiny—she could feel that something was still wrong with her precognitive perceptions.

Destiny rarely fought. Her strength was no better than the average woman's, and she had little stomach for physical confrontations. She was much better at orchestrating a plan, and her temperament suited her abilities. In this case, however, events dictated that she take a more direct role in the final act of the Brotherhood's plan. She carried a weapon for those rare occasions when it might be necessary to use it: a small crossbow—not well-suited for battle against Wolverine or Colossus, but more than sufficient to put an end to Senator Kelly's life.

Or, for that matter, to finish what Mystique had started in the hall outside. In the anteroom, Professor Charles Xavier and Doctor Moira

MacTaggert both lay incapacitated—but they would not remain so forever. Mystique believed them useful pawns in whatever game was to come. To Destiny, they were the enemy, and enemies were to be eliminated. That was the only valid solution to a conflict such as the one between the X-Men and the Brotherhood.

If Mystique did not return soon, Destiny intended to end the lives of both Xavier and MacTaggert. She would not consider allowing them to leave the Senate office building alive. Mystique at times outplotted herself and therefore did foolish things. Destiny knew how fickle the future could be because she saw it changing from moment to moment around her, solidifying only a few minutes or hours ahead of time. She knew better than to plan too far ahead.

Or perhaps it was not that she knew better, but that she had no need of long-range planning because her short-term planning was perfect—usually. Since that morning, she had been plagued by a precognitive blind spot—an uncertainty like a quantum superposition, a particle of action that refused to settle itself onto one path or another. The feeling was even more intense now than it had been earlier in the day, as if its source was drawing nearer—or as if the moment at which that blind spot would move from the future to the past was close at hand.

Was Senator Kelly the blind spot? Was he the anomaly preventing her from getting a firm picture of the near future?

Impossible. Nothing Kelly had done felt the least bit unnatural to Destiny, either before or after he did it. He fit perfectly into every temporal-historical moment he occupied—which was one reason why he had to be removed from history altogether. Too many other dangerous possibilities and potential sequences radiated out into his matrix of futures. None of them were good for mutants.

Who, then? It was like asking a blind woman, such as Destiny herself, what color blindness was. There was no way to pin down the nature of the uncertainty, because its nature as an uncertainty prevented this. It was almost physically painful, this indeterminacy intruding into her precognitive sense.

At least there was only one indeterminacy. She was still very confident that the next few minutes would contain certain events very beneficial to the Brotherhood—and equally unfortunate for Senator Robert Kelly.

That sequence of events would begin soon after she cocked this crossbow and placed a bolt in the flight groove, while stepping quietly back into the shadowed corner diagonally opposite the office door...

The door opened and Senator Kelly rushed in, shutting the door and locking it. He pulled his phone from the pocket of his suit coat and dialed. "Kelly here," he said, crossing the office to his desk and pacing in front of it. "I made it to my office. I don't think they know I'm here... yes, the damn mutants! All of them! What's going on outside?" He peered past the closed curtains out the window. Destiny stood patiently in the shadowed corner at the other end of his office, behind the couch and chairs he used for meetings and photo ops. "I can't see anything but smoke out there. Well, hurry! I can't wait in here all day. If you don't round them up, they'll find me sooner or—"

He saw Destiny then. "You're going to hang up your phone now," she said.

"They found me," Kelly said, and ended the call. He put the phone on his desk, straightened his tie, and faced Destiny. "Go ahead, then, coward," he said. "Do what you came to do."

"I will," Destiny said. "My colleagues have been defeated, but victory will be ours."

"Murdering me will accomplish nothing. People will fear mutants just like they fear any other terrorists, yes—but they won't be cowed. They'll fight back. They'll destroy you."

"Possibly," Destiny said. On that point, she was in fact uncertain. It lay too far in the future for her to make a decisive prediction, especially with the irritating kernel of uncertainty fogging her understanding. "But you are a greater threat alive. You may try to evade this bolt as I fire it if you wish, but I will know which way you intend to move before you do."

"I know who you are...*Destiny,*" Kelly said, scorn twisting her name. "I wouldn't give you the satisfaction. If I could kill you with my bare hands, I would. But I won't run."

KATE Pryde watched this exchange from her hiding place in a small alcove behind Kelly's desk, where she had pressed herself up against a low bookshelf underneath a globe. The alcove was partially obscured by a large, hanging American flag. Kate recognized Destiny. They'd crossed paths a few times during the fraught years following the passage of the mutant-control legislation, when the Brotherhood had kept up its fight against the X-Men despite the increasing threat to all mutants. Later, Kate had walked by Destiny's grave in the camp hundreds of times. There was an unsavory irony in her knowing Destiny's destiny, when the precog herself did not.

And on that topic, why did Destiny not know Kate was there? She should have known that Kate would try to intervene, but she gave no sign of being aware of Kate's presence. That made no sense—unless Destiny was playing dumb in order to spring some kind of trap, which seemed an unnecessary complication in an already complicated plan. Or unless Kate was somehow invisible to Destiny's precognitive sense because of the temporal projection. Could that be? There was no way to know.

Destiny smiled. "No," she said. "You will not run. You are a hatemonger and a despicable human, but you are no coward. Let that be your epitaph."

Her finger tightened on the crossbow's trigger, and Kate made her move.

She sprang forward, phasing through Senator Kelly's body. She heard his gasp—and felt it as well, sensing the twitch of his diaphragm and the sudden expansion of his lungs as she passed through him. She heard the sharp twang of the crossbow's string. As she emerged head-first from his chest, she solidified the parts of her body that were no longer occupying Kelly's space—and the crossbow bolt that would have punched through his sternum and into his heart struck her instead.

Kate tried to make a sound, but could not. Phasing had always made her acutely aware of the minute sensations of her body, inside and out, and this time was no exception. Even as shock flooded through her system, she felt the length of the bolt's shaft—from its entry point just under her right collarbone down through where its head had come to rest just touching the wall of her heart's right atrium. She fell the rest of the way through Senator Kelly, hitting the floor without feeling the impact.

Destiny was screaming, as if Kate's viola-tion of her plan had caused her physical pain. Perhaps it had: If her precognitive sense was part of her, damage to it could be like damage to sight or hearing. That thought flickered through Kate's mind and was gone.

There was a rushing in her ears, or maybe in her mind—she couldn't tell which. She felt like she was falling.

KATE smelled smoke and felt the light start to change. She felt unstable, as if she had a case of synaesthesia so bad that all of her senses had merged together. There was a curious doubled sensation to all of her perceptions, too—as if in addition to figuring out which perception fit which sense, she had to sort out

—which of us—

was having which perception.

Some tidal force drew her out of the teenage body so gravely wounded on the floor of a dim office in a burning building at a point in history where even precognitives did not know what came next…

…back to what? To the South Bronx? Back to

humiliating searches and everyday debasements and the looming prospect of nuclear annihilation? Back to being one of the last of her kind?

Kate met herself.

But it's your time, Kitty said. *How did you do this? Rachel's dead.*

She is? Kate replied. *How did* you *do this? I didn't...oh.*

Oh what?

You're in for a shock when you get there.

But you're going to let me come back?

It's not up to me. Did you...?

I don't know. There was...I don't know.

There's something you're not telling me.

I was about to say the same thing to you.

Touché. Are they still calling you Sprite?

Yeah. Not my idea.

I know. I always hated Sprite. You know what name I liked?

What?

Shadowcat.

Oh. Kitty paused. *I like that, too.*

KITTY rolled over and felt something grind against her collarbone. She cried out and saw, standing over her, the figure of Senator Robert Kelly. He was staggered, leaning on his desk for support. He stared as if he could not understand how she had come to be where she was—which, of course, he could not. Kitty Pryde—Shadowcat!—was not one of the X-Men he could have known about.

At the other end of the room, a woman dressed in pale blue was screaming, on her knees with her face buried in her hands and the backs of her hands pressed into Senator Kelly's office carpet. Kitty had no idea who she was.

Senator Kelly knelt next to Kitty. "Who are you, child? How did you…what did you do?"

Kitty moaned, then cried out as she tried to move. *You're in for a shock when you get there*, her older self had said. Something had pierced her shoulder, pushing deep into her chest. She couldn't breathe, but she wanted very badly to cough at the same time.

"You saved my life, little girl," Senator Kelly said. "I can't thank you enough."

"I hope you'll remember saying that, Senator," came a voice from Kelly's windows. Kitty looked up and saw Storm floating in, an arch smile on her face.

The tender expression left Kelly's face. "It's true, Storm. Credit where credit is due. That changes nothing about the nature of the mutant menace."

"Mutants, like any other people, are good and bad. You would do well to remember that, Senator. A mutant would have killed you today, had another mutant not saved you. Do not be so quick to condemn us all."

"Words to live by, Senator," Professor Xavier said as Moira MacTaggert wheeled him into the office. Both of them looked haggard. MacTaggert was using Xavier's wheelchair as a support.

"Professor Xavier! Doctor MacTaggert! Thank heavens you're all right," Kelly said. He was instantly the politician again, as if he had not savaged the two of them in the hearing chamber less than an hour before.

"We are well…or as well as can be expected. One suspects we would all be dead had Kitty not intervened," Xavier said, looking at Destiny. Her screams had subsided; she was in a near catatonic state. "Storm?"

Storm had gone to Kitty's side. She helped Kitty sit up. The wound around the bolt bled freely, and Kitty's face was ashen. Storm said, "Sprite, are you…?"

"Not Sprite…" Kitty said. Her eyes seemed to be having trouble focusing.

Storm looked more closely and dropped her voice to barely above a whisper. "Kate?"

Kitty shook her head. "She's gone back."

Storm looked over at Xavier. He nodded. "We need to get you treated," she said to Kitty. She picked the girl up, amazed at how little she weighed, and stepped to the window. "The world saw mutants fighting to save you today, Senator Kelly."

"And mutants trying to kill me," he said.

"Which ones were victorious?" Storm said. She had intended it to be a rhetorical question—and so it remained, as she lifted herself and Kitty out through the window. Then, picking up speed, she flew toward the Blackbird, waiting on the ground below.

He will never be our friend, Xavier said in Storm's head. *But we may have slowed his progression to being a deadly enemy.*

Maybe we have, Storm thought. *Please tell Logan to be ready for takeoff immediately.*

I will also have a discreet doctor ready in the Blackbird, Xavier said. *Kitty is doubly in shock, both from the time dislocation and from her wound.*

Television cameras followed Storm across the Mall, tracking her progress. She could imagine the reporters speculating about the identity of the costumed figure in Storm's arms. "Kitty," she said. "Stay with me, Kitty."

"Shadowcat," Kitty mumbled.

"What?" Storm asked.

"That's what she called me…"

Storm started to ask who Kitty meant, but she had a feeling she knew. She didn't want to pressure Kitty, but she needed to keep the girl focused and aware. Already blood streaked the yellow parts of her X-Men uniform—Storm could feel it cooling on her own skin as she rushed through the skies over Washington, D.C. "What was it like?" she asked.

"The worst thing I've ever…nothing could be worse." Kitty's eyes widened. "You, Storm. I was there when you…"

"Hush," Storm said. She burned, however, to know the rest—and know it now. After Kitty had had a chance to recuperate, she might decide some memories were better kept to herself.

"Everyone died," Kitty murmured.

"Hush, Kitten," Storm said. "Hush." Below, she saw the Blackbird. They were nearly there.

HANK McCoy, the blue-furred mutant known

as the Beast, looked after Kitty in the Black-bird's medical bay. Logan sat in the pilot's chair. Storm, Colossus, and Angel clustered close around. Xavier sat nearby, at the front end of the passenger compartment.

Nightcrawler brooded nearby. Since his encounter with Mystique, he had barely said a word.

"Well, what's the verdict?" Logan asked. "We saved Kelly, we put away four out of the five Brotherhood members, we made some great TV—but did we win?"

"I'm not sure what it would mean to win, Logan," Storm said.

"Beg to differ, Ororo," Angel said. "I'm pretty sure we did. Not permanently, but a lot of people who saw what went down today are thinking they need the X-Men. Know why? Because someone has to protect them against the Brotherhood. Everyone hates monsters until they need a monster on their side."

"I think it would be better if they did not think of us as monsters at all," Peter objected.

Angel nodded. "Sure would. But that's not the world we live in, Pete."

"We can gripe about this world all we want," Logan said. "But from the sound of it, what Kitty saw was a hell of a lot worse."

That was undoubtedly true. None of them was sure about how much of Kitty's muttering to believe—but if even half of it was true, Kate Pryde had actually *minimized* the horrors of the future she came from. New York in ruins, overseen by armies of Sentinels against a fiery sky—it was apocalyptic. Kitty had slipped into a fugue from shock and blood loss before Hank got her stabilized, and they were still trying to piece her story together.

"So Magneto controlled the Sentinels?" Logan said. "Figures. We should have made sure that guy never came up once he went in the ocean."

"I think you have it wrong, Logan," Angel said. "Isn't she saying he showed up and destroyed them all?"

"Not what it sounded like to me. But if that's

what happened, hey, I take it back." Logan didn't look convinced. The truth was none of them had a complete understanding of what Kitty had gone through, and they wouldn't until she could give them a clearer account.

"The part I can't figure out is your pet army of Canuck guerrillas," Angel said. "You planning that now?"

"You're their first target, bub," Logan said.

"The banter is natural in the aftermath of something like this," Xavier said. "But let us focus on what we need to understand. All those Sentinels had to come from somewhere, and very few currently exist. Who is going to begin the new construction program, who will finance it, and when will it begin?"

"All things considered," Angel said, "I think we came out of this pretty well. The Brotherhood's debut was not exactly successful, we all looked good on camera, nobody died, and now we have a lead on where a huge threat to all of us will come from."

"When you put it like that…" Peter said.

All of them looked out the window at the approaching airstrip. From the back, Kitty said, "Ugh, I hate landing."

Kurt got up and rushed back, putting an arm around her. "*Kätzchen*, what are you doing up? You have to rest." She leaned on him for support and he walked her forward, settling her in a seat next to his as they all buckled themselves in for the descent. She was pale and shaky, but he admired her desire to return to the team, despite the severity of her wound.

None of them said anything for a while. Kitty had been ripped from her own body, placed in an older version of herself living in a future that even Robert Kelly could not have imagined, and then torn from that future and returned to her body just in time to experience the near-fatal penetration of her heart by a crossbow bolt. Such an experience would have been difficult for anyone to handle, let alone a thirteen-year-old girl with very little experience in the kind of…unusual situations the X-Men tended to encounter.

Finally Hank McCoy spoke. "I'm more of a biologist than a doctor, but I got her stitched up. She's young, healthy—pretty soon she'll be doing cartwheels again."

"How about backward handsprings?" Kitty asked.

"Give it a few days," Hank said.

Silence fell for a while, until Logan said, "We oughta be on the ground again in a couple minutes. Everybody buckle up in case I crash."

"I don't remember everything I said to you, Ororo," Kitty said. "Did I make sense?"

"Yes and no," Ororo said. "Take your time. Futures aren't determined in minutes."

"Chaos theory would suggest otherwise," Hank said. "But hey, don't listen to me. Pete, why would they listen to me?"

"Good question," Colossus said. "I try not to."

"Did I really say Magneto had controlled the Sentinels? I don't remember it that way now,"

Kitty said. "That's not what happened. He's the only reason I came back. I think."

"You were having some trouble putting words together, Kitten," Storm said. "We'll get it all figured out soon enough."

"Maybe it would be best if we didn't," Kitty said. "I don't want to know. Except I do. What was she like?"

Everyone knew what she meant. Peter looked out the window. He was the other member of the team who was going to have a difficult time assimilating the implications of the temporal projection. Storm saw it, and knew she would have to take steps to make sure he did not just bury all of his emotional responses inside his stolid Russian frame.

Xavier also saw Peter's reaction and stepped in before one of the team had the chance to say something unfortunate. "Kate Pryde is as delightful and admirable a person as Kitty Pryde. The rest you will discover in due course."

"Do you think her plan worked?" Kitty

asked. She looked from one of her colleagues to the other. Behind her, Hank sat down and buckled himself in, too.

"No way to tell," Angel said. "Is there, Professor?"

"I do not know, Warren. Cliché though it sounds, only time will tell," Xavier said.

A minute later they were on the ground. Kitty managed to walk on her own down the steps. Hank led her into Xavier's mansion, where he could continue her treatment. Nightcrawler helped get Xavier's wheelchair down from the Blackbird. When the rest of the X-Men had gone ahead, he said, "Professor. What does it mean?"

Xavier understood, but he wanted to hear Kurt say it. "What do you mean by 'it'?"

"I had never seen anyone anything like me until today," Nightcrawler said. "But she was—"

"Kurt. You cannot answer that question today. Perhaps you will not answer it tomorrow. But you *will* answer it, if you stay with the people who fight with you and care about you."

Inside the mansion, Kitty stepped up to Peter as he came through the door. "I know it's weird," she said. "But don't worry about it. That might not even be this future. Rachel wasn't sure."

"Yes," he said. "I do not know Rachel, but I agree with her. We cannot know the future until we live it."

"Still, it makes me sad," Kitty went on. "Kate went back to that future—and when she got there, everyone was gone. She was the last one."

"That is only what was going to happen before today," Peter said. "After today, we cannot know."

"No," Kitty Pryde said, "I guess we can't." She shrugged reflexively, and then winced as the motion tore at the stitches Beast had put in her shoulder. "Ouch."

She walked with Peter and Logan and Ororo and Warren deeper into the mansion. She knew that, by saving Senator Kelly, they had changed something. But she also knew they might never discover exactly what that something was.

"It's not easy, not knowing," she said.

"Gets worse when you start thinking about

all the stuff you don't know," Logan said. "Stick to what's in front of you, kid."

That seemed like good advice.

EPILOGUE

SENATOR Robert Kelly knew how to grand-stand, but the truth was he did not enjoy it. A month after the disaster at the hearing, he had decided that more subtle methods were required. He'd convened a series of meetings, spoken with experts, even reached out to Charles Xavier again for a sub-rosa conversation about Xavier's goals for the mutant race. Xavier had argued that they were all the same race. All mutants—those who formed the X-Men and those who chose the Brotherhood—were part of the family, as it were. Kelly had conceded the point.

Others, however, would not have. Kelly was in the company of several like-minded thinkers now, each of whom had made room in very busy schedules. They had all agreed to meet in his office, away from cameras, in the very space where mutants had both threatened and saved his life.

Kelly was perfectly willing to admit that both things had happened. Further, he was willing to admit that not all mutants were bad. The actions of the X-Men were proof of this.

But neither of those facts altered his belief that the mutant menace was the most dangerous threat facing humanity, a crisis in need of decisive and ruthless action. An individual mutant might save a life, certainly. But the existence of so many mutants who desired the end of normal humans—or who, like Magneto, wanted to subjugate normal humans and rule them? That was a fact that could not continue to exist unchallenged. Robert Kelly prided himself on taking a fact-based approach. In this case, the facts were clear.

The implications were equally clear. Humans had to take action on their own behalf.

Four men were in Kelly's office, including Kelly himself. Another was his good friend, the President of the United States. The President was not as implacably opposed to mutants as Kelly would have liked. But he was a man whose heart was in the right place, and he was not unduly encumbered by intellectualism. He was not stupid—Kelly had found him to be intelligent and quite agile on topics that interested him—but he also did not see the value in overthinking a question.

Kelly respected that position. In fact, he shared it. Some things were complicated. Those things required intellectual agility and careful decision-making. Some things were simple. Those things required direct and forceful action.

The presence and growing power of mutants was the simple kind of problem. Their increasing militancy, represented by the Brotherhood, made the problem urgent. Kelly had survived the assassination attempt, but a number of people had died that day in the Senate building and out on the Mall.

"I won't bandy words, gentlemen," the President said. "I've read your report, Robert. Its recommendations are dangerous. They may be unconstitutional, which we could perhaps get away with, and criminal, which we probably could not—at least not in the long run. It is a draconian proposal, I must say, for someone who owes his life to the X-Men."

"A life that was threatened initially by other mutants, Mr. President." Kelly knew he had to be careful. Like all presidents, this one did not like points made to him too forcefully. "If there were no mutants—period—my life would not have been threatened at all."

"This is not just about your life, Robert," the President said. "It is about theirs, as well. There aren't many mutants, but they are citizens. They have rights. And they do have their partisans. Nevertheless—"

"There is also the national-security aspect, sir," added the third man in the room. "An anti-government group of super-powered beings, mutant or otherwise—or such a group in the service of a foreign enemy—would be a serious threat to our nation."

This man—Sebastian Shaw—stood apart from the other three, who were all dressed in the Capitol Hill uniform of dark suit, white shirt, and tie in a not-too-bold red or blue. In contrast, Shaw wore a sheepskin coat over a vest and ascot that would not have looked out of place against the teak and velvet backdrop of a London gentlemen's club. Kelly had known him for years, mostly as a donor but more recently as a kindred spirit.

Shaw was an industrialist, inventor, and—most important—a thinker along the same lines as Kelly when it came to the mutant problem. He knew that the actions of individual mutants, good or bad, were less important than the broader problem of mutants' existence. As long as there was a population of mutants, with powers no normal human could hope to have, they would be a threat to humanity. No interaction between groups with such a great power differential had ever turned out well for the weaker group—and after the assassination attempt a month ago, Robert Kelly knew better than most what it meant to be a member of that weaker group. Mystique had made the point quite clear in front of a worldwide television and online audience.

What could close that gap? Technology.

The President knew this, too. "I realize that, Sebastian," he said. "For the moment, our actions—my actions—will remain covert. The operation is code-named Project Wideawake. Allow me to present the man who will head it."

The fourth man in the room was unknown to Robert Kelly. He stepped forward as the President introduced him. "Henry Peter Gyrich. He'll be reporting directly to me. His first priority will be to work with Shaw Industries. Together he and Sebastian will make tremendous advances in counter-mutant security technologies. Our finest minds will dedicate themselves to the task."

"You'll have the best systems humankind can create, sir," Gyrich said. His fiery red crewcut and sunglasses, worn even in the shaded environs of Kelly's office, marked him as a Washington outsider as much as Shaw's sheepskins and crushed-velvet vest. Kelly knew little about Gyrich. He was a National Security Agency analyst with a whispered reputation as a hard charger, the kind of man who made his bosses' lives miserable until they either fired him or did what he wanted. And because he was very good at what he did, he got what he wanted much more often than he got fired.

"You also have my word that this mutant controversy will be resolved," Gyrich went on. "If we find them a threat to this republic and the human race, they will be dealt with. Permanently."

Their statements made, the four men sat at the couch and chairs where a month before a mutant had lingered, waiting for her appointed time to kill Robert Kelly. "Sebastian and I have known each other for some time," Senator Kelly said. "And you and I, Mr. President—well, we're not strangers, either. But I don't know Mr. Gyrich."

"Henry, please."

"Henry, then. Do you, Sebastian?"

"Never heard of him before just now," Shaw said.

"Well, Washington's a small town, so I've heard your name, and I know you a bit by reputation, Henry," Senator Kelly said. "Maybe we could get an introduction to how you plan to proceed? Executive-summary style, no need for details."

"Happy to provide it," Gyrich said. "But let's keep it quick. We've got a problem to handle, and it's not going to go away from us talking about it."

"Understood," Senator Kelly said. "You can skip right to the part about the new generation of Sentinels."

"That I will," Gyrich said.

THE OBSERVER in Senator Kelly's office was unseen, just as she had been the last time she entered this room. Although, Kitty Pryde mused, the last time it had been *Kate* Pryde who had phased in through the wall and waited for Destiny to ambush Senator Kelly.

Where was Kate now? Kitty wondered. What had it been like for her to reappear in the future, with the Baxter Building crashing down into a mountain of flaming rubble? Had she lived another day? Kitty wasn't sure, but she thought the Sentinels' communications link had been destroyed. Perhaps the impending nuclear strike had been delayed. Perhaps Europe and Asia and Wakanda would send help now.

But Rachel and Franklin and Logan and Ororo and Peter were all still dead. And Magneto? It was hard for her to believe he could have survived the fireball—but if anyone could have, it would be Magnus. She liked thinking of him by that name, something she had only confided in Professor Xavier because she knew he would understand perceiving Magneto as both friend and enemy.

She still wasn't sure Kate had made a difference. As Professor Xavier had said, they would not know until they lived their histories, and there were no shortcuts through time. Or, if there were, those shortcuts tended to disappear, as had happened when Kitty and her adult self had switched places.

Professor Xavier had debriefed her for a full week, trying to learn as much as he could about this potential future. "If we can learn what to watch for," he had said in his sitting room, "we can take steps to avoid that particular future—assuming it is possible to do so."

"Would we just make it disappear?" Kitty asked. "I mean, I was *there*. Will that never have happened?" She was lost in thought for a moment and felt Xavier's feathery touch on her mind. "Stop," she said.

"My apologies, Sprite. I thought to learn what was bothering you without disturbing your reverie."

"What's bothering me is…well, now you already know." She'd been irritated, and despite her reverence for Professor Xavier, she hadn't tried to hide it.

"Yes, I do. Perhaps I can help. Whatever happened in that future will exist as long as you exist to remember it. The courage and sacrifice of those future X-Men will not be lost. That may yet be our future, but if it is not..." He trailed off.

"If not, what?"

"The future we live is not the only possible future. There are thousands, perhaps, created from different chains of probability, choice, and action. At least, that is what seems to be indicated by your experience. Does that help?"

"If by 'help' you mean create a whole new set of confusing and unanswerable problems, sure."

Xavier smiled. "Glad to be of service. Now. Soon we will need you back in the field again, putting your unique abilities to use."

"I'm ready to go," Kitty said. "And by the way, can you not call me Sprite anymore? I'm Shadowcat."

The faintest hint of a smile wrinkled the corners of Xavier's eyes. He knew why. He and Kitty Pryde were the only people on Earth who did. "Very well. Shadowcat," he said.

NOW KITTY was doing her part to stop that future from happening. She believed Xavier, that altering their future would not unmake the one she had seen. It could, however, mean they did not have to live it. The idea was difficult to get her head around, but Kitty was beginning to feel more at home with it. She listened to the conniving bureaucrat Gyrich begin his description of Project Wideawake; she heard Shaw propose early plans for his next-generation Sentinels; she saw Kelly and the President exchange looks and nod their approval at each other.

Professor Xavier had said they would have to live their future to find out what it held. Kitty Pryde was fine with that. But she alone among them had already seen a future, and she had no plans to experience that one again.

We saved your lives, she wanted to say. She wanted to appear in their midst and strike terror into their hearts, saying, *We are mutants, and we are everywhere, and you can hide nothing from us unless we permit it to remain hidden*. But they wouldn't listen. She knew that. They would use such an act as one more pretext for what they were intending to do anyway. So Shadowcat stayed in the shadows and listened, and hoped she could use what she learned—this time—to save her friends.